Jobs in a Jobless World

☐

**WHERE THEY ARE
AND HOW TO GET THEM**

Jobs in a Jobless World

WHERE THEY ARE
AND HOW TO GET THEM

Godfrey Golzen

Frederick Muller Limited London

First published in Great Britain in 1983 by Frederick
Muller Limited, London SW19 7 JZ.

Copyright © 1983 by Godfrey Golzen

British Library Cataloguing in Publication Data

Golzen, Godfrey
   Jobs in a jobless world.
   1. Work
   I. Title
   331.1   HD4902

   ISBN 0-584-11048-0
   ISBN 0-584-11069-3 pbk

Printed in Great Britain by
Redwood Burn Limited, Trowbridge, Wilts.

Acknowledgements

A great many people gave their time in allowing me to interview them and in some cases also providing me with privately circulated documents and information. My thanks are due to all them – and my apologies to those I have accidentally omitted from the following list:

Chris Glover, The Institute of Directors; *Ron Ashton*, The Daily Telegraph; *Hugh Roc*, Chubb's Ltd.; *Professor Hunt*, The London Business School; *Phil Churchill*, PER; *Lucy Gaskill*, New Ways to Work; *Jim Smith*, MSL; *Leslie Robinson*, Forty Plus; *Trevor Austin*, British Airways; *Denis Bruce*, Manpower; Don Lueck, Intex; *Douglas Llambias*, *Piers Wemyss*, PA Consultants; *Jack Barnes* and *Genie Hart*, Minster Executive; *Charles Walker*, Charles Barker; *J. Fuller*, Personal CV; *Peter Bennet*, ASTMS, *Dermot Hoare*, Eurosurvey; *Robert Baird*, Baird Publishing; *Jean Harding*, SIAD; *Kenneth Lander*, Chusid; *Sir John Trelawny*, Korn/Ferry International; *Ted Simpson*, Sanders & Sidney; *Tom Carew*, Percy Coutts & Co.; *Keith Standring*, APEX; *Louise Botting*, Douglas, Deakin, Young; *Michael Armstrong*, Book Club Associates; *Graham Waters*, Executive Standby; *Michael Wood*, Search & Assessment Services Ltd; *Mrs A. C. Scott-Brown*, Interexec; *Tony Milne*, CEPEC; *Colin Hamilton*, STC Ltd.; *Dr R. Lessem*, Urbed Ltd.; *John Kellet*, Personal Counselling and Executive Careers; *K. S. Perks*, Wandsworth Resource Centre; *Roger Stacey*, Astron Appointments; *Terry Fuller*; the staff of the BIM Library.

Thanks are also due to *Tom Golzen* for re-searching and reporting on the problems of younger job seekers and to *Ann Golzen* for typing large parts of the manuscript.

Contents

Part One

FINDING A JOB

1. Putting It In Perspective

Statistics have never quite recovered from the slur, variously attributed to Disraeli and Mark Twain, that there are lies, damned lies and statistics. There are plenty of them about in the job market and they make depressing reading for anyone looking for a job or thinking of leaving one without another to go to. Three million unemployed; an average rate of unemployment in the UK of 15 per cent, a picture that is little better if you look overseas and likely to get worse before it gets better; or, say the pessimists, worse before it gets worse. Is this a reality, or are these statistics on the same level as those which in 1900 predicted that by the end of the century London would be submerged in horse manure?

The truth, as usual, is relative, though the present figures at least are absolute enough. It depends, for one thing, where you live – unemployment is 20 per cent in Northern Ireland, but only half that figure in the South East. It depends further on age, skills and, sadly, race. It is also attended by a good deal of mystery. Why is it, for instance, that with the building industry particularly hard hit by unemployment, it is so very difficult to get any kind of building work done? Could it be that there are people languishing on the dole but with another and healthier existence in the Black Economy? It probably could, if the loss to the Exchequer of £3–3½ billion a year in undeclared tax liability – the official guess – is anywhere near the truth.

The minority, resourceful enough to cheat the taxman and the National Insurance, are not the problem, though. They are the survivors. Reading a book like Jeremy Seabrook's *Unemployment*, a stark account of conditions in the post-industrial wastelands of the Midlands and North one cannot sustain any illusion that real poverty is an invention of the bleeding heart left. However, the plight of blue-collar workers without skills or with obsolescent ones is not within the scope of this book. It is aimed at professional and executive workers whose problems are of a different dimension except in so far that to solve them requires, in both cases, strategies for adaptation and survival that are divorced from a lot of traditional preconceptions about job-finding steps and career patterns. In the case of blue-collar workers, to overturn them needs new policies by both government and unions; for instance, on the part of the government more flexibility about the conditions under which people might be allowed to draw the dole and on the part of the unions less of a knee-jerk reaction that any change in working practices such as job sharing is an attempt to water the workers' beer. These are not matters which can be addressed directly in a book – at least not one which also gives practical guidance to managers, executives and professional people on how and where to find work.

Another way in which their situation is different – and in a sense which is less gloomy than that three million figure suggests – is in its scale. Consider how the three million unemployed are divided up:

    9.2% are 'managerial and professional'
    6.5% are 'other non-manual'
    12.6% are 'clerical and related'
    15.1% are 'crafts and toolroom'
    29.8% are 'general labourers'
    26.8% are 'other non-manual occupations'
(figures supplied by the Department of Employment)

It would be even more useful if these percentages could be 'broken down by age and sex' as the old demographic joke has it, but an analysis of which age bands are most affected by unemployment is not available from the Department – though it should be. One has to rely on hearsay and the information given by consultants in close touch with the market is that the people who find it most difficult to get jobs are those who are over 55 and under 28 and who have no specific qualifications in 'hot' areas like information technology. Overall, however, as far as managerial, executive and professional jobs are concerned (which we will refer to here as AB jobs), the number of unemployed is not 3 million, but under 300,000. That is bad, but it is not a static figure. The Report of the House of Lords Select Committee on Unemployment (1982) says that 300,000 vacancies are filled every month and one can assume that around 9 per cent of those are also AB jobs – that means that 27,000 people are getting an AB job *every month*.

On the other hand, there is a discrepancy between this figure and the statistics for the number of jobs advertised in the quality national dailies and Sundays. They vary somewhat according to source, but the needle hovers somewhere around the 40,000 a year mark[1] There is obviously a huge gap between this and the 250,000–300,000 AB jobs filled annually which one can imply by putting together the AB unemployment percentages and the monthly total of vacancies filled according to the House of Lords Report. So who has got their facts wrong?

To some extent it is probably a matter of interpretation. The distinction between an executive or managerial job and a supervisory one is often not that clear; what some people would regard as being a job for an Indian, others might take to be one for a chief. Similarly, when someone registers as unemployed, they are automatically given an application form to fill up to put them on the professional and executive register (PER), if the official at the jobcentre considers that they fall into that category. But there are other reasons for the discrepancy which are much more significant for the job seeker at AB levels.

1. Many jobs are not advertised in the quality nationals, but in technical and professional journals and in local papers. One of the leading job-ad media now, for instance, is the PER's own weekly freesheet *Executive Post*. It advertises about 450 jobs a week, many of them not shown elsewhere. (You get *Executive Post* automatically if you are on the PER register – but you don't necessarily have to be unemployed to get on the register. PER simply functions as a government-owned recruitment agency and you can put yourself on their books even if you're 'just looking'.)

2. A very large number of jobs are *never advertised at all* and this trend is growing. At the highest levels (£25,000 a year plus) it is estimated that at least 80 per

cent of jobs fall into this category. Even at the junior and the middle management end of the spectrum the percentage of unadvertised jobs is reckoned to be around 50 per cent.

The unadvertised job market is not just a new name for the old boy network, the 'it's not what you know, but who you know' syndrome. It is a new, far reaching, positive phenomenon that offers considerable opportunities for the alert job seeker at all levels and ages. Very little has ever been written about it. In a later chapter we describe in detail how it operates and how you can get into it by setting up your own listening posts and by piecing together bits of information which are sometimes trivial in themselves but, taken together, amount to powerful unadvertised job leads.

Indeed, a large part of this book is concerned with taking you behind the scenes of the conventional job market and showing you how it really operates. The point is that getting a job nowadays is no longer simply a matter of using the right techniques: organising the job search, writing CVs and letters of application, handling the interview and, ultimately, negotiating the terms of your next job. These things are important and we certainly will not neglect them, but if that were all there was to it, more people would succeed more quickly with the job search because there are now plenty of books and courses around that teach you to do that. But in a highly competitive market you have to be a jump ahead and one way to do this is to put yourself in the shoes of the man or woman who is sitting on the *other* side of the desk. What will make him or her say first, 'I've got to see that one'; then 'I'd better put that one on the short list'; and finally, 'I think that's the person for the job'? It is by studying the answers to these questions that the professionals – career and placement consultants – make their living and a large part of the research of this book has been devoted to interviewing them, extracting as much of their 'tricks of the trade' as they are willing to divulge or accidentally reveal and studying their unpublished internal literature.

Somewhere between the ultimate consumer – in this case the employer of AB labour – and the placement consultant are positioned the executive search consultants, familiarly known as 'headhunters'. Their story is an interesting one too because they are commissioned by corporate clients to find executives, mostly at a very senior level. Nothing to do with job *hunting*, you might think. Not so. As a first step in their search, they have to interview their client, establish his needs and find out what sort of ship he runs. This is not just a question of the job and the money. What are the power structures? What is their style? Do they work an eleven-hour day or does everyone push off at five? Are you judged by your results or your accent? And so forth. These are the very questions the job hunter should try to establish as well – but in this case they have been put together by professionals and refined over years of experience. Once again, a good deal of time has been spent talking to headhunters, finding out their opinions of their peers and of other kinds of consultants and studying the guidance notes they issue to their own staff.

Finally, there are the people in firms – finally, because they make the final decision who to see from among those who have sent in letters, application forms or CVs. Sometimes these are received in their hundreds when a particularly tempting job is advertised or when the job specification has been too loosely written. A job advertisement, in fact, can reveal a great deal, often unintentionally, about those who have placed it and here again we are going to take you behind the scenes of what an advertisement can tell you about an organisation and what the job really is, as opposed to the label attached to it.

However, recognising that writing job ads is a matter for professionals, companies are increasingly using recruitment and selection consultants to do this for them, just as they are increasingly using the services of such firms to sort out a short list of candidates. This often presents the applicant with two very different interview hurdles, one professionally erected by a recruitment and selection consultant and a second one placed by a line manager, not even necessarily in personnel, whose often limited experience in interview techniques presents both opportunities and hazards to the candidate.

The various types of brokers between applicant and job all have their various axes to grind and make claims for the success of *their* method of operating in contrast to other forms of consultancy or indeed rival consultants in the same field. Some head hunters, for instance, claim never to talk to career counselling and executive placement firms.

They say that when asked by a client to conduct an executive search, they confine it only to people who are absolutely secure, happy and successful in their present job and, by that token, the tops in desirability; to which account of the situation, career counsellors are apt to react with an expletive best left deleted. Others, again, do work with career counsellors in the headhunting process certainly when it comes to highly specialised, technical posts, but choose them very carefully on the basis of criteria that are obviously very interesting to job seekers who may be thinking of talking to such a consultant themselves. Between consultants in the same line of business there are also some revealing views about what makes, say, a good recruitment and selection specialist – views which they would probably not offer to a job seeker, but which have been given freely to the writer and which provide useful insights to those passing through that particular part of the job-hunting net.

The concern of this book is, in other words, with the dynamics of the situation – how, by understanding the market and where you stand in it, you can put yourself in a position to *control* your options rather than to be pushed around by circumstances. Part of that process is to understand how the job and work scene has changed (the two are not necessarily the same), how that in turn has changed attitudes of both job seekers and employers.

It has also changed the nature of the choices before you. 'One door closes as another one opens', is an old saying sometimes offered to job seekers, and remarkably cold comfort it generally sounds like. The fact is, though, that the same circumstances that are threatening existing jobs and shrinking the orthodox job market are opening up opportunities in other directions. For instance, listening to the news the very day that I am drafting this chapter, there is an announcement of 7,000 redundancies in British Airways by the end of the year. The commerical that follows that same news item advertises an increase of services by a new private airline from London to the West Country. What on earth is going on? Simply this: a big organisation with huge staffs, world-wide offices in the best locations and a publicity budget to match (think of all those coloured posters and models of identical planes with different marking!) cannot afford to run a small-scale operation where the revenues are not large enough to sustain overheads that are incurred, not in Plymouth or Penzance, but in Moscow or Miami. One man's loss-maker though, may be another's profit opportunity and this is being realised throughout the country and indeed in many other developed economies.

There are people, let us be frank about is, whose chances of finding another orthodox job are slim. It may be that they are too old, though attitudes towards senior people are changing for the better. Too old at 40 is mellowing towards too old at 55. (This age problem is now equally worrying at the other end of the scale – too young at 25 is perhaps even worse in terms of social consequences.) It may be that their track record is too patchy or that they have changed jobs too often, or that they have soared too high too soon, or not high enough, quickly enough. All of these things are difficult to overcome in a highly competitive market where it is by no means uncommon for employers to have several hundred applicants to choose from.

In that case the orthodox job market may not be for you and the sooner you stop hurting yourself and possibly demoralising others by beating your head against a brick wall, the better. 'There is a world elsewhere,' says Shakespeare's Coriolanus when he is banished by the ungrateful Romans. In the job market that world is one of self-employment, or re-retraining for a different career, or freelance and consultancy assignments and perhaps of working abroad.

Moving into that world is often a matter of making a mental adjustment in the direction of a recognition that terms like 'work' and 'jobs' are changing their meaning. 'What we have is a job shortage, not a work shortage,' says London Business School's Professor Hunt, in discussing the anomaly that, whereas we have three million unemployed, it is amazingly difficult to get someone to come and do simple maintenance jobs around the house. 'The trouble is that people have this very fixed idea that a job is something you do from nine to five in an office. The moment you get over that preconceived notion all sorts of horizons open up.'

As far as AB jobs are concerned the problem is, of course, one of upbringing, class and what the neighbours will think. There has recently been a study of 'urban legends': stories that may or may not be true but whose word of mouth prevalence reflects society's most common anxieties. In America the recession stories are of PhD's 'pum-

7

ping gas' or driving taxis; this is taken as showing how bad things have got, not what a comedown it is for the people concerned. In Britain, the stories are of men pretending to go to work every day rather than tell their wives that they have lost their job. It is an alarming illustration of the way the two countries react to the same problem.

One way to overcome the inhibition about jobs and work is to accept the fact that there are no logical steps to a career any more. There are only moves that are logical in relation to the market and in relation to one's own development, needs and abilities. Dare one say, in relation to one's own happiness? In order to make sense of your next step – to be in control of it, rather than to stumble along in the light of a set of preconceptions – it is important to understand what these factors are in your life and how they relate to the changing world of work and jobs. Even if you stay in the orthodox job market, it is only when you have understood and come to terms with them that you can develop your job-hunting techniques beyond a set of wooden formulae.

[1] Source: Media Expenditure Analysis Ltd.

2. The Changing World of Work and Employment

A friend of mine once bought a remarkable postcard in a junk shop. It was sent to someone in England from Moscow in October 1917 and it says, 'We are having quite a mild autumn, but there seems to be a spot of bother in the streets.' Nowadays it seems almost unbelievable that anybody should write about the onset of one of the century's most significant historical events in this way, but revolutionary changes have not, except in the case of the atom bomb, announced themselves in a clap of thunder. They have sneaked up on us gradually, recognised by only a few people whose warnings have generally been ignored until suddenly everyone wakes up, wondering what has hit them. The leap in unemployment figures, rising in a couple of years from an 'unthinkable' 1.5 million to an equally 'unthinkable' 3.2 million is an event of this kind.

It is not confined to Britain: the situation in the UK is worse than in other countries, but only in degree. From as far away as affluent Australia the reports are that 'we are in danger of becoming two nations – those who have jobs and those who do not. Unemployment is approaching half a million' (*Australasian Express*, 13.7.82). Even in Japan, a country with almost a tradition of full employment, we are now told of the Ministry of Labour declaring a state of emergency 'because of the May ratio of 58 job openings to 100 job seekers, the worst for several years' (*Guardian*, 22.7.82). What they and we are said to be experiencing are the effects of a technological revolution that has been compared to the Industrial Revolution of the seventy years from about 1750 to 1820. If this is the case – and most commentators now think it is – then there is very little

hope that a change of government, or an upturn in the
world economy, will improve the unemployment picture in
more than a cosmetic way. It is a question of
governments – and individuals – looking at the economy
in a new way and adjusting to new ideas of work and
employment.

It will not be the first time this has happened. 'Watching
masses of peasants scything a field three hundred years
ago, only a madman would have dreamed that the time
would soon come when the fields would be depopulated,
when people would crowd into urban factories to earn their
daily bread,' says Alvin Toffler in his book *The Third
Wave*. At that time, too, people found their careers disrupt-
ed. In those days, of course, careers in the modern sense
scarcely existed, except in professions such as law and
medicine, but it was not only peasants in the field who
were affected. There were highly-skilled craftsmen and
tradesmen – perhaps the equivalent, in status, of today's
middle management – who operated from home in cottage
industries such as weaving. They were largely self-
employed, doing piecework on contract or supplying goods
and services to their community and, by the standards of
the time, they had a good and not terribly strenuous
existence; taking plenty of holidays and working or not
working more or less as their needs dictated. The new
technology of steam-driven machines changed everything.

Machines in mines, in mills, in steel and wood working,
indeed in all productive processes could and did work
harder, faster and more reliably than men. Factories
grew up around the engine. For the first time it was
possible to have many hundreds of people working in one
building purely for the reason that such a method was
more productive. The industrial revolution had begun.
Clive Jenkins and Barrie Sherman *The Collapse of
Work* (Eyre Methuen, 1979)

The craftsmen and many other skilled outworkers found
that they could not compete with machines. Their prices
were forced down to below subsistence level and, being
unable to beat the factories, they were forced to join them.

Employment in factories was a very different proposition
from sub-contracted self-employment or even from working on the land where the pace, though hard, was still

determined by the seasons, the weather and the light.
Factory conditions were filthy, both in the workplaces
themselves and in the towns that held them and which
grew in decades from villages to conurbations with hundreds of thousands of people living in them. The work was
heavy, monotonous and, compared with the past, highly
disciplined. Obviously, when you had machines you could
not work at your own pace or take time off when you felt
like it. It was only by making a virtue of necessity and
calling it 'the work ethic' that you could persuade people to
accept the deterioration in the quality of their lives that
the Industrial Revolution entailed.

The work ethic, closely tied up with religious belief, was
not just a drug peddled by the middle classes to persuade
the workers to accept their miserable lot, as some left-wing
historians assert. The middle classes, who to a large extent
were made up of people who had emerged from the ordin-
ary workforce, passionately believed in it for themselves as
well. There was a general acceptance that steady, regular,
disciplined work was a good thing and that, by and large it
meant taking or giving employment rather than individual effort. Only a minority of artists or professional
people worked in the old, pre-Industrial Revolution way.

As modern economies were formed, working conditions
gradually improved, but even though machines became
more powerful and sophisticated, the basic principles of
industrial labour did not change very much. The work
ethic was unchallenged. It might even be said that among
its staunchest and most conservative defenders was the
trade union movement itself. The concept of 'the right to
work' is not new and one suspects that it is upheld not only
because it is the key to earning a wage, but because it also
embraces the dignity and status that is attached to steady
and regular employment. 'Amidst the overwhelming
reasons for wanting to work,' say Jenkins and Sherman –
incidentally leading officials of the left-wing union
ASTMS – in their book, 'there was the underlying philoso-
phy that one *needed* to work.'

In the middle quarter of the twentieth century, economies were increasingly directed by government policies
and it became possible to solve periodic employment problems by the measures advocated by Lord Keynes in his
General Theory of Employment, Interest and Money, published in 1936. Keynes thought the best way to tackle the

problems caused by the slump, when unemployment in the UK at one time rose as high as 22 per cent, was to stimulate the economy by boosting public spending. This in any case occurred naturally – as it were – with the outbreak of the Second World War and it continued throughout the post-war period, when both governments spent money freely to establish and maintain the welfare state.

By this time, in the words of Jenkins and Sherman, 'Keynesian heresy had become Treasury orthodoxy' but the doctrine was sharply challenged in an influential series of articles by two Oxford economists, Eltis and Bacon, in the *Sunday Times* in 1976. They put forward the view that the public sector had become an enormous fat cat, sitting on top of the British economy. Its virtually unsackable employees bullied governments into inflationary wage settlements because of their monopoly position in many key industries. These, in turn, fuelled leapfrogging pay demands in the private sector and when jobs were lost there because of the poor competitive position that resulted, the unemployed were simply mopped up by being given more jobs in the public sector. Eltis and Bacon pointed out that the growth periods in Britain's faltering economy were getting shorter and shorter because productive industries were simply running out of labour almost as soon as any upswing in demand got going.

The corrective, as supplied by Milton Friedman and the monetarists, was to cut government spending right back and to create a market economy in employment. One man's pay increase was to mean another man's redundancy, unless there was also an increase in productivity to pay for it; no more state handouts, as the Tory press of the time put it.

Since the beginning of the huge increase in unemployment coincided with the introduction of this tougher attitude to public spending, the tendency has naturally been to lay the blame on the government. Certainly their policies have had something to do with it, as indeed has the dislocation of the world's monetary system caused indirectly by the various oil price fluctuations. But the real culprit is the new technology. Vast numbers of jobs at every level from the shop floor to the boardroom are no longer needed; or, if they are, they will have to be done in a radically different way. If a future government was to reflate the economy drastically, traditional forms of employment could not be brought back from the dead; indeed it might only make the rich employed minority richer and the poor unemployed, poorer.

Theoretically, of course, the new technology makes all things possible – a Utopia where everyone works shorter hours for the same money and there are still huge profits left to be taxed and steered towards a general improvement in the quality of life. Certainly, this is the vision held out by Jenkins and Sherman in *The Collapse of Work,* but, attractive though the idea sounds, there are some fairly major political, economic and psychological obstacles in the way. 'By the year 2000, the working week will have become a three times eight-hour hour day,' they prophesy. They go on to say, 'This system, which will have to be adopted internationally, would obviously imply both a decreased labour productivity and decreased profits.' In other words, countries and individuals will have to agree not to compete with each other – not to sneak in, say, a four-day rather than a three-day week and thereby undercut the competition or meet a deadline. Can anyone really see this happening? And where will the investment to pay for this fully automated world come from if, as they suggest, 'Unemployment pay must be paid at around the national average. There must be no financial penalty attached to being workless'?

It all sounds like some kind of economic Indian rope trick and the reason is that although Jenkins and Sherman challenge traditional views of work, they still think of it as synonymous with regular paid employment and are contemptuous of any attempt to formulate alternatives. An ASTMS spokesman, interviewed in connection with this book, dismissed encouragement of small businesses as being, 'a drop in the bucket – window dressing which is quite irrelevant to the problem of three million unemployed'.

Is it though? We will return to the subject later, but the point of introducing it at this stage is to show the prevalence of the attitude that the alternative to unemployment is orthodox employment, presented in this case as being to work less hard at the same things, rather than to work in new modes, like self-employment. And if that sort of scaled-down work is not available, then the state must somehow provide. In other words, if we are to sin against the work ethic, we must be given absolution at least in the financial sense: 'there must be no financial penalty attached to being workless.'

Not that the Tory government's solutions are any more promising. There is some dim recognition, or perhaps only a hope, that small businesses might provide an answer, but steps towards creating new work patterns of this kind by intelligent, pump-priming public spending are taken hesitantly. Instead there are a great number of palliatives: YOPS (Youth Employment Programme), CEP (Community Enterprise Programme) and TOPS (Training Opportunities Scheme) to name but three out of a selection of twelve employment schemes listed in a series of articles which appeared in the *Sunday Times* in 1982 by their economics editor, Mary Hogg. All these schemes are, like those of the unions, based on the notion of creating employment, particularly in the manufacturing sector. It would be foolish to dismiss them on 'drop in the bucket' grounds, but one can only agree with Jenkins and Sherman when they say 'these expedients can at best only be regarded as short term and based on the premise that sooner or later unemployment will go away'. They are not that dissimilar from a highly informal job creation scheme recently witnessed at an hotel in Eastern Europe – unemployment is by no means confined to the industrial West – where a seeing eye beam opened the lift automatically, but an attendant with a device like a tennis racket was employed to activate the beam whenever a guest approached to use the lift!

It is, of course, possible to be vastly pessimistic about the future of worklessness. Some commentators say that our troubles are only beginning, that by the end of the decade the unemployment figure in the UK will have risen to five million and that the rest of the world will be similarly affected. It is just possible that the political consequences of such a situation could lead to some sort of international work limitation agreement on the lines put forward by Jenkins and Sherman, though the lack of anything other than talk at SALT (Strategic Arms Limitation Talks) does not augur well for such a solution. A more realistic scenario will be one where the economic self-interest of the manufacturing firms and nations take a hand. When Walter Reuther, the American trade union leader, saw his first industrial robot his comment was, 'They don't buy cars'. Millions out of work means the loss of millions of customers and the only way out of that dilemma is either to subsidise the unemployment out of taxation or for *new* forms of work to be established. To help with the latter must surely be more to the taste of industry than, in effect, to pay for the creation of customers through taxation. But how can this be done?

Some very interesting ideas on the subject are to be found in an excitable, but often exciting book by Alvin Toffler, called *The Third Wave* (Collins, 1980). Toffler believes that we are entering a second Industrial Revolution where the application of the new technology will enable consumers to specify and get exactly what they need. The result will be 'a demassification of marketing, mechandising and of consumption', a process already foreshadowed in the rise of mini-magazines, newsletters and small-scale, often xeroxed communications along with the coming of cable, cassette and the computer'. One effect of Third Wave production will be to bring work back from the traditional workplace to the home: into what Toffler calls 'The Electronic Cottage'. He says, 'One can picture the work-at-home family of tomorrow inviting an outsider or two to join in – for example a colleague from the husband's or wife's firm, or perhaps a customer or supplier engaged in related work or, for that matter, a neighbour's child who wants to learn the trade. One can foresee the legal incorporation of a family as a small business.' The customers of this kind of enterprise would be larger businesses sub-contracting part of their operations, like writing computer programs or providing after-sales service; or they would simply be individuals in the community who wanted goods and services tailored to their particular needs and specifications. There may not be many of them about at the moment, but once something appears on the market for which there is a demand, that demand soon takes off. Who would have thought, in 1970, that the pocket calculator would become an almost universal possession? It would be in the interest of both government and industry to encourage such activities, because, in the words of Toffler, 'Additional spending by one person means additional income for a host of second parties . . . these people then spend their additional income on more goods which benefit yet more people.' The increasing interest being shown by big business in the various business resource centres being set up throughout the country indicates that the lesson is sinking in.

Another interesting aspect of Toffler's argument which is relevant to the theme of this book is his suggestion that we need to re-define what is meant by work. 'During the First Wave (before the Industrial Revolution) most people consumed what they themselves produced. They were neither producer nor consumers in the usual sense.' They were what he calls 'prosumers'; that is, they consumed quite a large part of the goods and services they produced themselves. According to Toffler, this sort of work – DIY, for instance – was downgraded in the Industrial Revolution and after. Yet who can doubt its real value to both the personal and the national economy? 'Once we recognise that much of our so-called leisure time is spent producing goods and services for our own use ... then the old distinction between work and leisure falls apart.' Thus Toffler sees the emergence of a workforce which 'might well earn less – but compensate by supplying their own labour for tasks that now cost money'. He goes on to ask, 'Is a laid-off worker who puts a new roof on his house or overhauls his car unemployed in the same sense as one who sits idly at home watching football on television?'

Is this all blue-sky stuff, some kind of futurologist's heaven? On the contrary, the evidence is that, like the Russian Revolution in our first paragraph, such a process is already in our midst. Toffler points to an example with which everyone is familiar. Up to the mid-sixties motorists would have been amazed at the thought of filling their own tanks when they bought petrol. Now it is almost equally unusual to find a pump that is attended. In one sense this has led to a loss of jobs among petrol pump attendants; it is equally certain, though, that it cuts a penny or two off the product. More significant, if less obvious (often because they are concealed in the Black Economy) is the enormous growth in 'second income' jobs. Researching a book on this subject in 1982 I was struck by the number and variety of jobs of this kind and the range of people – from seventeen-year-old schoolgirl to the wife of a wealthy merchant banker – who were engaged in them. I looked at a sample of thirty-five occupations, but it was clear that I could have multiplied it by four and still not exhausted a phenomenon that is producing all sorts of goods and services, from holiday accommodation to antique restoration, that may not exist in the orthodox employment market but for which demand has increased rather than diminished in the recession.

At this point you may be starting to say to yourself, 'Yes, this is all very interesting and may well be true, but how is it actually going to help me in my job search?' The answer is that a very large part of the job search, a very large part of the problem people have with finding work at every level has to do, not with the job market (though no one pretends it is easy) but with their own rigid attitudes towards what work is and how and where to go about finding it. This is true at every level. Jeremy Seabrook in his book *Unemployment* (Quartet, 1982) which is concerned with blue-collar workers, tells of a carpenter in the North-East who has been unemployed for several years since the shipyard where he worked closed down. A carpenter! Such a man could virtually write his own pay cheques in many parts of the country, yet he will not move to where the work is.

Other people will not change jobs for reasons of status. The downward move in the orthodox employment market is a tricky one and often impossible to achieve because of employers' suspicions for all sorts of reasons (including sometimes the potential threat to their own position) of the 'overqualified' candidate, but it is possible in some highly technical areas and there may increasingly be employers that offer it either directly or indirectly in the form of part-time work or job sharing. For instance, British Airways have recently trained surplus pilots as air stewards – a scheme that has been readily accepted by many younger men who have turned out to be less status-conscious and to place more value on the general aircrew lifestyle than their older colleagues.

This is a hopeful sign but, in industry at large, the sideways move is probably a more realistic possibility for those whose position is under threat. The personnel manager – a species whose jobs have suffered more than most from cutbacks and changes of attitude – may need to inventory his or her skills as an administrator, as a person with industrial law experience, as a welfare officer, as a communicator, as a negotiator and so forth and see if they can be applied to some other area or maybe in some other country. Indeed, anyone who has reached a plateau in middle management – and that again has turned out to be a high risk area at a time of technological change – might be well advised periodically to re-examine their skills and qualifications to see whether they are being applied or allowed to stagnate. In the latter case, a move in or beyond the orthodox job market might well be worth considering because the de-skilling nature of many middle management jobs is one of the most dangerous consequences from the point of view of the individual who, in all probability, will have to change jobs more than once in the course of his or her working life. An American book published some years ago, and called *The Peter Principle* first drew attention to this phenomenon in putting forward the view that people were always promoted beyond the level of their competence. The tendency is for, say, a perfectly sound chemical engineer to be appointed to a managerial position where he or she gradually loses touch with their own subject and gets involved in administrative matters at which they may turn out to be less competent or which are very specific to the organisation they are in; or both, which is even worse. Such a person might well consider a move back to familiar ground rather than remaining stuck on a plateau which is by no means the safe place it once was. 'Clerical, administrative and managerial posts and the whole information industry workforce are at risk,' say Jenkins and Sherman (presumably they mean the old-style information industry). 'Clearly not all the jobs, but some of all these types of jobs are threatened . . . all jobs which repeat one or even many operations and where personal decision-making is at a minimum or non-existent.'

Easier said than done, you might say, and of course you would be right. The orthodox job market is very, very tough – especially so for the over-50s, the under-28s and those who have been out of a job for a longer period of time. It is toughest for those who think it is going to be easy, because the let-down is so much harder. It is amazing how often one hears from consultants, counsellors and employers about job seekers at every level from newly-fledged graduates with an upper second or a first class honours degree to senior executives in the £20,000 a year plus range who think that their qualifications put them beyond the necessity of marketing themselves properly. 'Just before you walked in,' one headhunter said to me, 'I had a letter from a former chief executive who'd been earning £30,000 a year. There wasn't much indication of what he could do – only a handwritten CV, nine pages long. Now I ask you . . .' The sentence trailed away eloquently.

This person had probably read somewhere that if you send out your CV to as many prospects as you can think of – what one American book calls 'the numbers game' – something is bound to happen. This is about as intelligent as going to a place to fish if you have no idea whether there are any fish there at all, whereabouts they are or what bait they will take. You just might be lucky, but the odds are 1,000 to 1 against, or worse. In today's job market, if you are going for orthodox employment, you have to research your stretch of water very, very carefully – and, to continue the analogy, study the habits and feeding patterns not only of the species of fish but of the particular one you want to catch. Just replying to advertisements is like joining the ranks of the hopefuls who stand together in rows, beating the water in the hope of getting a bite. How often does one ever see them catching anything?

It is also a question of being flexible in your attitudes and your tactics. In America there has been a rash of new-style books on job hunting whose eccentric titles – *What Color is Your Parachute?* or *Guerilla Tactics in the Job Market* – reflect that following courses of action that relate to the old, stable career patterns is no longer an adequate way of tackling the problem. You still have to know what you want in order to get it, but in establishing what that is you will have to discard a good many assumptions, if they stand in your way: about status, about career patterns, about where you are prepared to work, about what the neighbours will think, about what your parents and peers expect of you and, above all, how you actually set about the job search. The world of employment is no longer going on in a predictable way. The kind of unstable conditions we now have – and are likely to have for the foreseeable future – call for a great deal of resourcefulness in your search, the clues to which are, as we have shown, firstly to stop thinking of employment and work as being necessarily synonymous, as they were in work ethic days, and secondly to think of jobs as being simply what crops up in the 'Appointments' pages.

Whether this process leads you to explore and look for growth areas of the orthodox job market by discipline, product or geography, or into variants of it (like working part-time and substituting, from your own labours, for goods and services which you would otherwise have to buy), or into its fringes (like going freelance) or into the growing opportunities for self-employment which spin off from the new technology depends on the conclusions you come up with as to how your needs, skills, abilities, qualifications, resources and circumstances relate to what is 'out there'. We will deal with this in a later chapter. But let us first of all consider some of the more immediate problems connected with finding a job in a jobless world – like, should you do so at all if you are now in a job? And if so, when? And if you have no option in the matter, how can you make the best of things – for instance by browbeating/shaming/persuading your employer to give you the best possible deal?

3. Moving in Today's Job Market

Making a move in today's economic conditions – and they may well be with us for years to come – is not something to be undertaken lightly. Given that you have any option in the matter, in what circumstances should it be initiated at all? Clearly, they fall into two categories. The first can be ascribed to pressures from within – the feeling that the money or the prospects are not good enough in a firm, a chosen career path or a geographical area. The second is still voluntary but might be triggered by a certain amount of duress. Some sort of signal has been made and you would be foolish – or think you would be foolish – to ignore it. There may be an overlap between the two as well. An inadequate salary may reflect what someone is considering to be an inadequate work performance. But on the whole, internal pressures are less immediate than those from the outside and therefore need to be looked at critically. 'Is your journey really necessary?' as they used to say in World War II posters; because it will seldom be an easy one, particularly if you time your departure badly.

Money

The money for the job fills two functions. In the first place it enables you to 'make a living' as the phrase goes. It also has a symbolic value in that it indicates where you are in your firm or profession and how your skills are valued by those whose job it is to reward them. 'On the face of things,' says a well-known consultant, 'if you're earning 15 per cent less than the going rate for the job – that is the rate that is usually attached to a similar package of functional responsibilities in a firm of a similar size – then you're being underpaid.' He went on to point out, though, that it is generally difficult to make comparisons of like with like.

'In highly taxed western economies it's become customary to wrap up quite large chunks of remuneration in the form of perks and fringe benefits. People tend to forget that in comparing their salary with that of a similar post in another company. The company car, the company credit card and the company "contracted out" pension scheme – to name just three of the many perks that are now quite common – are worth several thousand a year on top of the stated salary.' In fact, a very experienced career counsellor who in this context would no doubt prefer to remain nameless, advises people not to be deterred from applying for jobs that may appear to be above their salary league because if they count up the value of their fringe benefits they will probably find that their total remuneration was much higher than they thought. 'A £12,000 a year person plus company car is a £15,000 a year person, excluding a company car,' he says. In deciding whether or not money is a valid motive to look round for something better, what all this adds up to is that you should realistically assess what your perks are worth. By the same token, of course, if you are getting few or no perks in your present job, the actual reward may not be as good as the salary indicates.

Prospects

Every bright-eyed and bushy-tailed job applicant is advised to ask about prospects and it is usually a question that interviewers find very difficult to answer unless some kind of succession bait has been dangled in the advertisement: 'It is envisaged that the post will lead to a board appointment on the retirement of the finance director in two years time.' That kind of assurance is seldom given, however, and the usual move, when an employer is asked about prospects is for vague statements to be offered about advancement matching performance. Given the fact that people cannot learn a great deal about each other in an interview it is hard to see how they could do more. But if such a remark is made either then or at any other point in your working life, it becomes important to pin it down: what advancement, meaning what in terms of power, position, money or whatever you have set your heart on in return for which performance? Some American career counsellors in fact advise that such promise made or prospect held out should immediately be confirmed in writing by its recipient. This may look a little aggressive on occasion – whether it is appropriate depends on one's own feeling for the style of the organisation within which one is working – but certainly anything said on these lines in a job interview should be clarified in an acceptance letter if a job offer is received. Misunderstandings do happen. One firm of my acquaintance went through three group chief accountants in five years because although the prospect of a board appointment was held out at the interview, the level of performance for that promotion was not made clear. The inevitable result was anger and confusion when it began to look as though this particular carrot was always going to be kept out of eating reach.

Significantly this happened in a smallish family company and it is here that 'prospect problems' most often occur. Such firms tend to be run autocratically by one person with no clear organisational structure and no great accountability except to family shareholders. They are often pleasant places to work in and there may be a trade-off between this fact and other disadvantages. But if promises about career of financial prospects have been made and not kept, there is something wrong either with your performance or with the organisation. Either case is a warning signal.

Trouble at t'Mill

One reason why things are not happening as planned is often that the company is in trouble. Though it is suggested that it is only rats that leave a sinking ship, it is a pretty foolish rat who does not make at least some contingency plans if he has to run up a vertical slope to get from one side of the vessel to the other. While job prospects for someone made redundant as a consequence of a general closure are somewhat better than for those who have been picked out for redundancy, in today's conditions very few people without a specialist qualification will walk straight into another job: four months for the first £10,000 of your last salary, plus another month for every £1,500 a year over that is what many career consultants give as the time it takes to find another job. It is better to have that wait while you are earning than when you are on the dole.

This golden rule should also be observed by all those who are thinking of moving for all the other numerous reasons there may be: boredom, inability to get on with colleagues or bosses, a feeling of being out of depth in the job, tired of travelling or simply wanting to live in another part of the country. 'It is much more difficult to move when you are out of a job than when you are in one,' says Tom Carew, the immensely experienced head of the career consultants Percy Coutts Ltd, and his view is echoed by all other consultants in the business. 'Never let the word "resign" pass your lips, unless you have a job to go to,' said another counsellor who admitted that he often sent people who had walked out of their job and come to him for help with the advice that they should go back, withdraw their resignation and apologise. It is very difficult to swallow your pride, but it makes a satisfying meal compared to some of the alternatives. Besides which, while nobody will pay you to resign, it is possible to negotiate redundancy terms which will tide you over what might be several months of waiting.

Negotiating redundancy and severance

The statutory redundancy payments in the UK are clearly laid down in the Redundancy Payments Act and they are not all generous. The exact provisions are set out in leaflets on the Redundancy Payments Scheme which are available from places like jobcentres and Professional and Executive Recruitment (PER) offices. Suffice it to say that the maximum sum payable is £4,050 and to rate that amount you have to have had twenty years continuous service with the employer. If you have worked for him for less than two years you are not eligible for any redundancy payments at all. There is also a statutory provision for notice of redundancy or payment in lieu which is equally modest – a maximum of twelve weeks after twelve years of service or more.

That is all the employer is required to do by law and if you are unlucky enough to be caught in a firm that has gone into receivership – an increasing possibility these days – that is all you are likely to get. In that case the money is paid out of the government's redundancy fund and the liquidator or receiver should send you a leaflet produced by the Department of Employment called *Employee's Rights on the Insolvency of the Employer* which outlines the procedures to be followed. If you are owed holiday money or back pay (in some small firms there have been cases where, immediately before collapse, not even salaries were paid out) you receive preferential treatment over other creditors, but not necessarily the full amount due. Finally, there are many arrangements the employer may have made to pay out over the statutory minimum for redundancy – more on this in a moment. This would be regarded as an unsecured debt and you are unlikely to get more than a tiny percentage, if anything.

The liquidator should send you two forms, IP 1 and IP 2, on which to make your claims. However, in making plans for your immediate future you should reckon with the fact that it may take some considerable time before your claim is met. An article in the *Sunday Times* in August 1982 pointed to delays of up to eighteen months before full settlement was made and nine months was not uncommon.

The inadequacy of the statutory redundancy payments scheme has meant that a wide variety of topping-up arrangements have appeared, some of them developed with the unions as formal redundancy procedures. These are mostly in larger firms and if you are employed by a company that has such an agreement your personnel department would obviously have made you aware of it. However, the vast majority of companies, while generally treating people who have been made redundant more generously than the state scheme does, have no clear-cut scale of compensation laid down. In fact, the person who has been landed with the unenviable task of breaking the bad news to you will probably have been given a range of parameters to work in, rather like a job offer in reverse: 'offer X but don't go higher than Y'. In that situation it helps you enormously to know what the precedents elsewhere are. Merely to protest that whatever you are being offered is less than you had hoped will not produce much of a response. To be able to say that it is less than the settlements negotiated by white-collar unions like APEX or ASTMS will have some force – irrespective of whether or not you actually are a union member (though in this situation it may well help if you are) – because no employer likes to tangle with the unions even at times of high unemployment. Indeed, it is the policy of many employers to offer better than the union rates in order to keep the unions away from his firm.

If a deal on redundancy is being offered to you, do not jump at it immediately, even if it sounds good. While the employer does not *have* to offer you more than the statutory rate, in all probability he or she will be feeling desperately embarassed about the whole thing – certainly so if you have had years of satisfactory service at executive or supervisory level. They would like to 'do the decent thing' and if you keep your head you will usually get a better deal than if you say yes right away. Even if you have been expecting the axe to fall, your first response should be to say that it is a great shock and that you would like time to think the offer over. If it really has come as a shock the need not to panic is even greater.

So what can you reasonably expect? Starting at the top end of the market, Chris Glover of the Institute of Directors is often asked by companies and individuals what a reasonable settlement would be.

It depends on a number of factors. One is whether or not the parting is amicable. Then there is the age of the person, length of service, position and, nowadays, the company's financial state. At director level the settlement should be six to nine months' pay. A person in their fifties who's been with a company for ten years or more should get a year's pay at least. Then there's the question of fringe benefits. Some companies are generous about allowing people to keep their car or buying it at a cheap rate. Often they will go on paying BUPA, for a while at least. In the case of older executives they may pay a lump sum into their pension scheme – there are often tax advantages attached to paying compensation that way.

Apart from direct payments, career counselling is increasingly being offered as part of the redundancy or severance package. Though there are free courses given by PER to help redundant executives, the service given by the various counselling firms is more thorough – but it's not cheap as far as the individual is concerned because he can't reclaim the VAT and he can't charge it against tax. A company can do both. The cost comes out at 12½%–15% of their last salary.

Some firms also arrange for financial counselling. The tax position on larger golden handshakes can be very complicated and specialist advice on tax avoidance devices can be very beneficial in some cases. Even if tax considerations are not involved, expert advice on how best to invest your money in the circumstances is always a help.

Another way of smoothing the thorny path of redundancy at senior and long-service levels which appears to be gaining favour is to offer part-time consultancy to the person affected as part of or even in lieu of a golden handshake. Whether such an arrangement is a good idea depends on your tax position. Only the first £25,000 of any golden handshake is free of tax and a part-time consultancy may be a handy way for an employer to help you avoid tax by spreading part of what is effectively a termination payment over a number of years and in the form of earned income. On the other hand it may inhibit you from being as active as you should be in finding another job or in setting up some other form of employment such as self-employment – it may create a conflict of interest there, too, if you go into an area similar to that in which your part-time consultancy is already. 'It depends whereabouts in your career you are,' says one executive who has a three-year contract to do some part-time consultancy with the firm that took his company over and merged his division with one of theirs. 'If you're in the 35–50 age bracket and feel you want to move to another job or start something else, I wouldn't recommend it. It ties you down too much. But if you're in your fifties, it's quite a pleasant way of slowing down, particularly if you can combine it with another part-time job.' A consultant with much experience of counselling redundant executives warns, though, that such assignments should be set out as formal contracts. 'In some less pleasant firms, it can be a ploy for evading a decent settlement. They give the person a job to do which he or she can't really handle and then fire them for not doing it properly.'

At less senior levels it is useful to know what sort of deals the unions are getting from employers for members who have been made redundant. Interestingly enough, in terms of salary and notice, they are at least as generous as the Institute of Directors' informal and unofficial recommendations. Thus a model job-security agreement on which the white-collar union APEX (Association of Professional, Executive, Clerical and Computer Staff) negotiates with employers provides for nine months' notice for staff with over five years' service and six weeks' pay per year of service (seven weeks for people over 40) up to a maximum of seventy-eight weeks' pay. On top of that there is an 'unemployment supplement' of a week for each year of service in recognition of the length of time it takes to find another job these days. This, in fact, is a growing trend. A survey produced by ASTMS (Association of Technical, Scientific and Managerial Staff) on *Supplementary Payment Following Redundancy* shows a wide variety of schemes produced by both private companies and nationalised industries for making continuing payments for a while based on length of service to staff who have been made redundant; for instance ITT makes a hardship allowance of ten pounds a week for twenty-four weeks if employment is not found. Another document, produced by Incomes Data Services lists the redundancy/severance awards of a number of large companies. Between two and four weeks' pay per year of service, according to age, seems to be about the going rate in companies who report a formal procedure which goes beyond their statutory obligations.

The tax position

Comparatively few people who have been made redundant or otherwise lost their jobs are likely to have profound tax problems, now that the Inland Revenue's rather cumbersome procedures have been simplified. All termination payments have been lumped together and made free of tax up to £25,000. The only part of the severance package below this amount which is taxable are arrears of holiday pay.

Over £25,000 things get rather more complicated. In essence, the situation is that on any amount over £25,000 and up to £50,000 the 'golden handshake' part of your total income is taxed at half your normal rate and from £50,000 to £75,000 at a quarter of it. Should it exceed £75,000 you get no relief at all, but at those heady levels you almost certainly have access to the kind of sophisticated financial advice that finds holes in even the finest tax net.

In fact, where the payment of substantial sums is involved, it might be a good idea to get expert advice in any case – on both the investment and the tax implications, especially if you are planning either to take early retirement or use the money to start up your own business. The problem is first to catch your financial advice. The average accountant is not usually well versed in these specialised matters and the recommendations of some firms calling themselves investment advisers may not always be impartial. 'Ask who is paying the bill when you get financial advice,' says Louise Botting, a director of the Douglas

Deakin Young consultancy, who is also the lucid presenter of the BBC's 'Moneybox' programme. 'If you're not being charged a fee, the consultant is getting a commission on your investment – and the kind they put you into could be where the commission is fattest rather than the one that's best suited to your circumstances.'

Financial counselling does not come cheap – which is why it is a good idea to ask your company to pay for at least an initial session as part of the severance deal. Check out any consultancy you are thinking of using – and even more anyone that approaches you – with your bank or ask the advice of your own company's financial director if he or she is a person of sufficient calibre and judgment to be useful over such matters.

Apart from the problem of what to do with a lot of money, you may also need advice on not having enough – this would be particularly true when the financial collapse of an employer leaves you with nothing except a long wait for your redundancy payment. In that case you should discuss the problem with what are likely to be your two principal creditors – the building society and the bank. These days, when redundancy has become an everyday occurrence among their customers, they are likely to be accommodating about rescheduling your payments over a longer period. The important thing is that they should know what is going on, rather than be faced with your payments suddenly drying up. Ultimately, after all, the building society do not want to call in a mortgage unless there is no other way they can ever get their money. The same is true of the security on bank loans.

Unemployment benefits

There is a deep-rooted objection, not shared by the young for many of whom it has become part of their way of life, to signing on for the dole at the unemployment benefit office. This is rather illogical, since a regular proportion of your earnings, ever since you started work, has been deducted for national insurance contributions, part of which fund unemployment benefits. They are modest but useful – the rates are usually revised upwards every year and are set out in a DHSS leaflet (NI 196) which is available from social security and unemployment benefit offices.

You may not be eligible for benefit straight away however. If you have received payment in lieu of notice you

will have to wait until the period of notice expires before
you can claim benefit. Also, if you leave a job voluntarily,
you may not be able to claim benefit for the first six weeks
of unemployment. In fact, there is now some evidence that
when substantial termination payments are made, the
DHSS *attribute* part of this as payment in lieu, even
though the employer has stated that no period of notice
was given. If you want to question this or any other matter
concerned with benefits, you should do so with the super-
visor, not with the benefit office clerk. Insist on seeing him
or her, rather than getting into a row with a clerk whose
powers are strictly limited.

The general advice is to sign on for unemployment
benefit even if you are not immediately eligible. For one
thing it means that you will be informed of all your rights
immediately and there should be no delays once you do
become due to receive payment. It also puts your name in
front of PER – of which more later – and you can, if you
wish, enter their employment register and start receiving
their weekly freesheet *Executive Post* which contains some
400–500 job advertisements, mostly in the middle management range, in each issue.

Pensions

In the private sector, very few people indeed stay with one
employer for the whole of their working lives. In fact, the
number of times they move around between the ages of 25
and 45 has probably increased and three or four job
changes during this period are more common than not.
Possibly because the legislation on pensions was drafted by
civil servants who tend to remain in government employment until they collect their index-linked entitlement, it
has failed to provide at all satisfactorily for the harsher
realities of life in the private sector. There has been much
talk of changing the legislation to correct the anomalies
and sometimes the hardships that it can cause, on retirement, to people who have changed their jobs too often or at
the wrong moment, but because of the complexities of the
matter, many experts think it will take years before
anything is done about it.

These same complexities also tend to deter executives
from thinking about pensions until it is too late. Putting it
as simply as possible, the position is as follows. Since 1978,
employers have been obliged to provide a pension scheme

which, on retirement, produces *earnings related* benefits in addition to the very meagre *flat rate* state pension. Both employers and employees contribute to the earnings related scheme which, in the case of the one run by the state, provides on retirement at 65 for men and 60 for women, 1/80 of final salary for each year of service up to a maximum of twenty years. There is, however, an alternative. Employers can set up their own private scheme, provided that the benefits this offers are at least as good as those of the state scheme. Because the latter has a number of disadvantages, a great many employers – probably the majority – have chosen to go the private road – what is known as 'contracting out'. Typically, a contracted-out scheme will be more generous than the state one ('contracted-in') and provides 1/60 of final salary for each year of service, with no maximum. For instance, if your final salary was £15,000 and you had been with the company for twenty years, you would receive an annual pension of 20/60 of £15,000: £5,000 a year. You may, of course, receive much more than that, depending on the generosity of the employer.

The problem, though, occurs when you decide to leave before retirement. Only if you are under 26 and have been in the scheme for less than five years can you take your cash contributions with you – note *your* contributions. Those of the employer remain in the scheme and you lose them. If you decide against this course of action, or have no alternative because you have already been in the scheme for more than five years, you keep your employer's contribution as well as your own *but* your pension is 'frozen' and you cannot collect on it until you retire.

Supposing you are now 35, have been with a company for ten years and are now earning £12,000 a year. You are entitled to 1/6 of £12,000 – £2,000 a year, *but only when you retire*. What will this sum buy in thirty years' time? It is anybody's guess, but no prizes are awarded except to the pension companies who get the interest on the money until you retire. They claim, of course, that their rates take account of such swings and roundabouts.

The obvious answer is to transfer your pension to your next employer but this is not as easy as it sounds. No two pension schemes are exactly alike and it is difficult to put a value on contributions made to dissimilar schemes producing different benefits on retirement. However, unless you can persuade your next employer to accept a transfer of your old scheme you are likely to lose out badly. Supposing for instance, that you make your last job change at 45 and that your salary at retirement will be £50,000 – a possibility which inflation makes by no means unlikely for only an average flier. Your employer at that time will only want to pay you 20/60 of £50,000. For all the other years all you will get are bits and pieces of pension frozen at levels which by then may scarcely pay for a month's groceries.

There is not at present a great deal you can do about this unhappy situation except to be aware of it and, in negotiating your next job, to try and get your employer to take your present pension scheme aboard along with you. How successful you are in this will probably depend, at least in part, on whether your move is voluntary or not – another reason for either planning your move in good time or, if it is an involuntary one, for getting financial counselling put into your severance package.

The Perils of Paranoia

Not very long ago, a friend of mine was appointed to a highly paid newspaper job. The paper was presently rumoured not to be doing well and the gossip was that this was due to the editor. It was not long before he and my friend were at loggerheads and she found her position increasingly intolerable. She was advised by all and sundry to 'hang in there' since the paper's by now well-publicised troubles made it likely that the editor would be asked to go before she was. In that case her difficulties would be resolved one way or the other. Either she would be able to establish a better relationship with his successor or she would be paid off with one of those handsome severance awards that are common in Fleet Street. She did not take the advice. She resigned on a Friday. The following Monday the replacement of the editor was announced. Happily she got another job within a very short time, but the story also shows that resigning at the wrong moment can be a very expensive gesture.

The question is whether one should resign at all and as we have heard earlier the answer is usually no, unless you already have another job to go to. There are, however, signs and indications that should be heeded. Cyril Marks of Percy Coutts and Partners says:

If you get the feeling that things are not going right you should start your job search straight away, even if some tempting non-job is being offered to you. A skillful selection consultant can spot a meaningless assignment in someone's CV a mile off.

The range of such assignments is infinite – usually they consist of being removed from a really functional job to some reporting or consultancy task of no great importance. A real life example (necessarily altered here) appeared on one company's noticeboard as follows:

From May 1st James Blower will relinquish his duties as departmental head in order to concentrate on assessment and development at director level. The marketing managers reporting to him will each become responsible for all operational matters relating to their own divisions.

There are, of course, many other ways of indicating to people that it is time they started looking round. According to Professor Hunt of the London Business School:

One thing you ought to look out for is not being invited to meetings. Then, when you find out that a meeting has taken place which you ought to have been asked to, the ploy is to tell you it was 'just an informal get-together.' Or you may be denied information or personnel or equipment needed to do your job properly. Or someone gets appointed to the division you're in charge of without your being consulted. Assassination by rumour is quite common too. Someone puts about the story that you're not the man you were.

According to Michael Korda, author of *Power in the Office* (Weidenfeld, 1975) this last is quite a common ploy:

Gossip can be used to spread bad news before it's officially announced in order to make the actual announcement less painful and surprising . . . The gossip system can be used to warn someone who's going to be fired in order to facilitate the task of the executive who has to do the firing and also serves as a means of warning people whose performance is unsatisfactory.

Korda also believes that some of the signals can be physical:

> The first sign most people have that their future employment is being 'discussed is that they're quarantined and ostracised. People greet them a little too heartily, but, while doing so, carefully cross to the other side of the corridor in order not to get too close.

This is not to suggest that you should start a paranoid hunt for adverse signals at work – merely that one should be realistic about the fact any executive is vulnerable if they feel they are no longer quite on top of their job, if there is a serious downturn in profits in some part of the organisation for which they are responsible, or if some new factor like merger or takeover has entered the situation. If the signs are there, it is unwise to ignore them, hoping they will go away or believing that 'it can't happen to you'. As Michael Korda says in his book:

> It never does to forget that managements, like individuals, get bored with what they have and since they are not anxious to replace themselves for the sake of change, they can only change by shaking things up below them.

References and Rows

Counsellors report that, when people lose a job, some are depressed and others are angry. On being asked which he thought was the healthier reaction, Leslie Robinson of Forty Plus had this to say:

> 'I'll show the bastards' is a good reaction if it means that you intend to prove them wrong by your subsequent progress, but a bad one if you're thinking of litigation. You never win in those circumstances. It takes up an enormous lot of time which should be spent job hunting and usually a lot of mud gets slung some of which is bound to stick to you. Generally the employer can carry on a legal battle far longer than an individual. Also, even if you do win a wrongful or constructive dismissal case, the awards are not that high unless you really have been the victim of some monstrous injustice.

The general feeling is that there is little to be gained, and often quite a lot to be lost, in going out in a blazing row, however tempting the prospect sometimes seems. Indeed, it may be wise to part on as good terms as the circumstances allow because a prospective employer may well approach your previous one for a line on you. If you are failing to get jobs which you feel should have come your way a discreet enquiry on what is being said about you may be in order. Spite is fortunately rare but it does on occasion arise and is very difficult to track down, though a career consultant might be in a position to do so. The laws of defamation are fairly strict and if you have evidence that defamatory remarks are being made about you, this is one area where a discreetly conveyed warning to the person concerned can at least neutralise a dangerous situation.

Moving Into Your First Job

All these hazards may fill the new entrant to the job scene with so much terror as to make him or her wonder whether it is all worthwhile and there is no disguising the fact that job stability, along with marital stability, has become the exception rather than the rule. So how can you manage the situation in such a way that your moves will be controlled by you rather than by circumstances? One answer is to pick jobs, right from the beginning, in occupations and careers which are likely to grow rather than the reverse. In very broad terms, Alvin Toffler in *The Third Wave* sees the effect of the new technology as being:

> Shorter product life cycles, more leasing and renting, more frequent buying and selling, more ephemeral consumption patterns, more fads, more training time for workers (who must continually adjust to new procedures), and more frequent changes in contracts, more negotiations and legal work, more pricing changes, more job turnover, more dependence on data, more ad hoc organisation – all of it exacerbated by inflation.

These views are borne out by the US Bureau of Labour Statistics which has identified the following growth areas of employment in the next decade:

– *Engineering*: needed at every level, from technician upwards. Mechanics, repairers, plumbers, carpenters: replacement and re-modelling will be, as now, boom areas.

35

- *Inspectors (manufacturing):* a sophisticated workforce will ask for increased safety standards, both at work and as consumers.
- *Credit and collection workers:* small businesses will need services of this kind.
- *Secretaries, typists and receptionists:* they will still be needed though their skills and tasks will be upgraded in the automated office.
- *Accountants and lawyers:* will be in demand to formulate and explain undiminished legal and fiscal complexities.
- *Personnel and training:* though presently hard-hit by the recession, tipped to make a comeback through the new skill of 'human resource development' (a phrase already beginning to appear in some job ads). This would represent a move away from the welfare, social science-oriented approach to personnel work which grew up in the sixties and seventies towards a more hard-nosed, quantitative approach to planning temporary and permanent personnel needs in relation to specific tasks and business cycles. Training people for the continuing flow of new procedures which Toffler has identified would also be important.
- *Information services:* there will be a move away from traditional and at present not very highly regarded areas like librarianship towards sophisticated forms of information gathering and retrieval.
- *Environmental services:* people will become increasingly aware of the need for measures to protect the environment.
- *Insulation workers:* there will be a big demand for energy-saving techniques in response to fuel shortages.
- *Paramedical services and medical administrators:* an ageing population, more and more medical technology and a decrease in the state's ability to fund medical care will boost the growth in private medicine that has already begun.
- *Police and security:* cities will become even less safe than they are now and crime will go on increasing.

No less important than picking the right industry or occupation is establishing whether you are putting your foot on the right rung in the career ladder within a particular firm. In some companies, for instance, all the top jobs are filled by engineers, in others by accountants. In publishing the tendency has been for senior management to come from the editorial side, for sales to have a relatively low status and for a move from sales to editorial to be rather rare. These are the sort of things you need to establish about your prospective workplace and the best way to do so is to talk to those in it, or who know something about the place. Particularly in smaller industries, gossip is rife and often informative.

There is also the question of broad aptitudes. It is a matter about which people even with work experience can be amazingly naive, sometimes, one suspects, because the media present a rather glamourised picture of certain occupations. One good way of putting at least some of your strong and weak points and your likes and dislikes to the test is in vacation jobs. You will seldom be lucky enough to land one in an area directly related to a career path in which you are already interested and you may well think that washing dishes in a restaurant, heaving boxes in a warehouse or pushing a pen in someone's accounts department has little relevance to a 'real' job, but it does contain certain lessons – your ability to deal with people from other backgrounds, for instance, or your capacity for doing tedious tasks quickly and accurately; an inevitable ingredient, you will find, of virtually any job. Certainly interviewers are always interested in your work experience and what lessons you think it has taught you.

Finally, and at the school leaver age, there is the opportunity of work experience in your last two years at school. How useful this is depends heavily on the firm you go to, though certainly well-organised ones like Marks & Spencer take it seriously. Even if you find it disillusioning, the experience is well worthwhile. It is, after all, better to be disillusioned before you commit yourself to a job or a career than when you are in it.

4. Life Crises and Your Career

There was a much discussed film two or three years ago which had the simple but evocative title, *Bad Timing*. It traced the sporadic relationship between a couple who were very much drawn to each other but whose paths always seemed to cross at what was, for one or other of them, the wrong moment. For this reason, each time they met, the outcome was an unhappy one.

Some people's working lives follow a similar pattern; they never quite seem to make the right move to the right place at the right time. To some extent this is a matter of realistic self-assessment, a topic with which we will deal in a later chapter, but it also has to do with understanding the nature of one's personal development. We are, after all, more than the sum of our abilities, skills and work experience.

The Mid–life Crisis

One such aspect has been well-documented – in fact it has long been established as a somewhat sour joke subject: the seven-year itch. The theory behind the seven-year itch is that a lot of marriages break up after some such period. People get bored with each other, limitations become faults of character, idiosyncracies become annoying habits and annoying habits become insupportable irritations. Some lucky people, of course, never go through this phase at all, others are able to cope with it wisely but in many cases they either break up or soldier on, becoming increasingly estranged, but afraid of breaking away in a new direction. The seven-year itch has been upgraded in recent years as the 'mid–life crisis', but that is not to doubt its reality.

Nor is it confined to marriage. Many people will recognise its symptoms as being equally applicable to their jobs at about the same point in their lives. They have reached the plateau of where their particular abilities will take them in that kind of organisation; for instance, they may be in a firm where advancement is only by filling dead men's shoes and nobody looks like dying for the next ten years. Or it may be that their work has become boring. There are careers which, after a certain point, seem to hold out no prospect other than doing more or less the same thing – if perhaps on a bigger scale and with more money – for the rest of your working life. That kind of realisation begins to dawn at about 35 or 40 and this is the dangerous age at which personal dissatisfaction coincides most frequently with job and career problems; indeed one may be mistaken for the other. 'That's the age at which a high proportion of executives get itchy feet,' says Sir John Trelawny, a partner in one of Britain's leading firms of executive search consultants and he goes on to add 'The first move is often a wrong one, particularly if it's due to psychological and personal pressures. When jobs are hard to find, a switch is not something to be undertaken without careful thought about objects or the real reason for wanting to move.' In other words, making a move is not the answer to personal problems, though the two are often closely related and therefore where you are in your personal development should not be neglected in planning the course of your working life – however sceptical you may feel about 'psychology'.

The Rebellious Twenties

It so happens that the 35–40 mark coincides with a difficult phase in people's sexual or marital state, but it is not by any means the only stage in your life where job and career decisions are liable to be affected by developmental factors; and vice versa. A widely discussed account of these phases has been given in the American book, *Passages* (Bantam, 1977) which is in itself a popularisation of a good deal of research into human development and behaviour. The author, Gail Sheehy, sees the early years of working life, from about 22–29 as being those where you push beyond the frontiers of your upbringing. You are apt to reject the values of your parents, the preconceptions you were brought up with and, in your working life, the limitations of the working environment – what Gail Sheehy calls 'the oughts and shoulds'. That is often liable to produce con-flicts over matters like behaviour when you clash with the accepted way of doing things, but it is also a very fruitful phase in many people's lives and one which organisations should maybe learn to use more effectively. It has been noted, for instance, that many Nobel Prize winners do their best and most creative work in those early years.

The Years of Transition

The next phase is one of transition, where you realise that things are more complicated than they seemed in your first impatient years. You discover that in work as well as in other aspects of your life the best way of getting from A–B may not be to draw a straight line. This is where you begin to become aware of office politics and that maybe there is a good reason for some of the practices and procedures that you questioned earlier. The experience of John, a young architect, summarises this:

> When I first went into practice in the early seventies I got impatient very quickly. They were doing a lot of work for local authorities – a bit of housing, the odd school, a police station – that sort of stuff. I wanted us to go in for international competitions, get our name around a bit and to take a look at prospects abroad. They just didn't want to know, even when the Middle East took off with the 1973 oil boom. They considered it but thought it was too risky. At home they knew what they were doing, knew the people, knew which wires to pull to get jobs and, of course, it was good, steady bread and butter income for the practice. When reports started coming through that some of the firms that had rushed out to the OPEC countries were finding it hard to get paid or getting hopelessly snarled up by local bureaucracies, my principals didn't exactly say 'I told you so' but the thought was certainly in the air. The irony of the situation was that in the end we were both right because towards the end of the seventies there were all these cutbacks in the public sector and work just dried up. We're doing all sorts of odds and ends now – interesting stuff, but nobody's getting much of a living from it. Maybe if I'd played it differently eight years ago, been more persuasive and less abrasive, I could have talked the partners into being a bit more adventurous. I suppose they took what I said to be an implied criticism of the way they were running things. Or maybe I should

have gone out on my own. I'm still working for them – in fact I'm an associate partner now. As things are at present, it doesn't look like a good time to set up my own practice.

The Settling-Down Years

John's story illustrates a whole range of ways in which stages of one's development influence one's career. Having got through the rebellious twenties, in the more reflective thirties he was brought face to face with the complexities of life inside and outside the office and the constraints they impose. He has entered, in his mid-thirties, into an acceptance of the established order of things. He has moved up to associate partner status and though the money is not brilliant he is probably doing as well as most people in his profession at his age. However there are some signs that may be the first symptoms of a classic mid–life crisis. He clearly feels that he missed a chance to break away at one time and now, when economic prospects are poor and he has acquired the usual commitment of a family and a mortgage, it may be too late; and as an associate partner in a practice that still has quite a prestigious name in the profession he has enough incentive to hang on. The crucial questions, as he nears his forties, are whether work will pick up and his financial position improve and whether he will become a full partner; and these in turn will accentuate, or be accentuated by, other factors in his life. 'Whatever rung of achievement he has reached,' says Gail Sheehy, 'the man of 40 usually feels stale, restless, burdened and unappreciated. He wonders "is this all there is?" He makes a series of departures from well established lifelong base lines, including marriage.'

Balancing on the Peak

In the next stage, from the early forties to the early fifties, John may well settle into the pattern which he found his principals were in when he joined the practice. He knows what he is capable of delivering, he 'knows what he is doing' in terms of his work, his marriage will have settled or he will have found another partner. (This whole pattern, incidentally, is largely the same as that experienced by working women.) These can be the most productive and most serene working years of one's life – they certainly were when we had stable employment conditions – because

41

confidence in one's own ability coincides with a move up to
higher salary levels at a time when financial commitments
to mortgages and education are lessening, when physical
restlessness – ranging from a desire to sail round the world
to experimenting with other sexual partners – has diminished, but when one is still young enough to enjoy life
to the full.

Unfortunately, these are now also the years when people
are most vulnerable in their career. They have probably
lost touch with some of their more marketable skills and
qualifications – the erstwhile biochemist has moved up to a
management post far removed from scientific research, the
one-time engineer will be selling six-figure projects at
government level – and though they have exchanged them
for experience, contacts and knowledge of the ropes, all
that is often very specific to one particular organisation.

At the same time the end of their career is still a long
way off – too far off for them to have achieved real financial
security in the shape of accumulated capital or an adequate pension. In any case, very few people want to retire at
that point in their lives. They may want to break out in a
new direction, but they have given too many hostages to
fortune – salaries, expense accounts, pension entitlements
and so forth – to up sticks and move on. They may also by
now have got rather set in their ways. They know – or
think they know – what can and cannot be done and what
that is is usually circumscribed by their own experience; a
self-fulfilling prophecy, in other words.

If you own your own business, or are a major shareholder
or partner, the only threat to your position is from the
world outside. What you think cannot be done may be done
by a competitor more in touch with the market, sharper in
his or her business methods or more ready to take a risk,
but nobody inside the organisation can tell you what you
ought to do. The matter is otherwise when you are an
employee, even at a senior level. This is sometimes overlooked by executives who after years of building up a
subsidiary at top level tend to think of it as being virtually
their own business. Dennis found himself at 52 shunted on
to the side lines by his firm.

When I took over the European operations of the American pharmaceutical firm who'd headhunted me at 38,
there wasn't much there except a bridgehead. I built the

whole thing up from that to a turnover of 30 million dollars a year. We have 200 employees and are highly profitable. Then they had a management change after a takeover in New York. The new people that came in were a bunch of youngish guys from Minneapolis and I don't think any of them has worked closer to Europe than maybe Philadelphia. They came up with a lot of damn-fool idea about opening a warehouse on the continent so that we could serve the Common Market better – as if London was much further from Rome than Amsterdam is. Really naive. We already had a highly efficient auto-mated warehouse on the South Coast with a twenty-four hour turnround. All this was going to do was to knock a great hole in our profits without really improving deliv-ery times, except maybe in Holland. I could see who was going to get the blame when it didn't work. It was a no-win situation for me, but when I put up my arguments against the move, it was obvious they didn't like it one bit.

Dennis was very much in the situation that John's principals would have been in had John come into the firm as a top appointment from some distant head office and forced their hand. He could not believe that he was being forced out after the contribution he had made to his firm's growth. In fact, he had identified with it so closely that he had really got around to thinking it was his own show, but without a shareholding his job as MD was no safer than that of the packers in his warehouse.

Was Dennis right about the idea of a warehouse in Holland? Only time will tell, but the point is that he *felt* it was not going to work. Had he been a younger man he might have been less obstinate, he might in fact have seen it as a way of increasing his firm's presence on the Continent. The people in America felt as threatened by his intransigence as he felt threatened and insulted by their implied criticism of his stewardship. Though it was essentially a dispute over a commercial decision, there were aspects of the clash that clearly related to the different developmental stages of the parties involved. These are the ingredients of many a 'resignation over policy matters'.

The Wise Elder Phase

From the point of view of moving around in paid employ-ment, the last years of one's working life are notoriously difficult. Nearly all types of consultants agree that whereas employers are much readier to consider candidates of around 50 than they used to be – often for the not entirely healthy reason that they want a person who 'can start on Monday' rather than a young graduate who might need some training – from the mid-fifties onwards placement becomes extremely difficult. The feeling is that older people tend to lose some of their momentum together with the shape of their waistline. Of course there is a certain amount of truth in this, but there are also compensating factors that are more recognised in other cultures. Jack Barnes of Minister Executive, a leading firm of career counsellors, has found that in some overseas countries the 50-plus person is looked at in a different light.

Increasingly, countries in Africa and the Middle East don't want young flyers. They have their own, or are bringing them along. They want an older man with experience. For instance, we've lately placed an engineer in his mid-fifties with a Middle East government who wanted someone to vet the work and tender applications of British construction companies out there. He's finding it varied, fascinating and very, very well paid. Never been happier. His employers know that at his age he is not likely to be lured away by a commercial firm nor is he likely to have to rush back home with family problems as happens to so many younger men out there. The point is that in Africa and the Middle East they're used to the concept of 'the wise elder'. He may not be able to hunt and kill any more – but he has a lifetime's experience to draw on – including his own past mistakes – he is not after the chief's job and he is not likely to take away the pick of the young men and start a rival tribe of his own. Somehow it's only in politics, where you are still young at 50, that we've accepted this principle in the West. Maybe things will change. It's certainly something we're trying to persuade companies here to see.

By the same token, though, senior executives should be aware of the relationship between their developmental stage and the kind of work they should consider: advisory, perhaps part time, guiding the hunter to his or her ground, but not actually themselves leaping about with war paint and spear. Even in terms of self-employment, often the only option for the older executive who has been put out to grass, it is important to stay within one's physical limits and, given a reasonable degree of security and diminishing commitments, this ought to be a feasible course of action.

Once again you may be saying to yourself, 'I can see the truth of all this, but how can it help me in practice?' The lessons are two-fold. Firstly, any problem you may be experiencing at work may have less to do with how you are actually performing than with a mismatch between your personal development and that of your superiors or the people around you: a case of bad timing, in fact. Secondly, and following on from this, in planning your job search, you will have to go beyond meeting the traditional specification based on such matters as job function, salary, age, location and so forth. Matching the job and the organisation to the appropriate phase in your personal development – or being adaptable enough to do it the other way round – is also important. The person in mid career may find the turbulence of the 'young, fast-moving company' (as it is often described in the job ads) an exciting new challenge – but he or she may also be swamped by it. Equally, someone in their twenties or early thirties might consider that to be trapped in a rather staid and conservative working environment could be to invite a bad case of mid– life crisis a few years hence, by which time moving on might be much more difficult.

5. Unpeeling the Labels: Self-Analysis and Self-Assessment

Making the right move in the job search or along the career path is not only a matter of where you are in your life and what stage of mental, and indeed physical, development you have reached. It is also a question of analysing why and where you have failed or succeeded, and drawing the necessary conclusions from that, rather than ploughing along the same old rut just because it is the one you know.

This approach to a problem is by no means confined to the job scene. Edward De Bono, in his famous book, *Lateral Thinking*, pointed out that people tend to think about problems in a very rigid way, determined and structured by all kinds of preconceptions and assumptions about how they ought to approach them. The solution was much easier to find when they were able to break away and see matters with a fresh eye. To illustrate what this means, there is a story about when de Bono himself was called to New York to advise on complaints that the owners of a certain skyscraper were receiving about the slowness of the lifts. The lifts were not really slow. The users only thought they were. De Bono's solution was to install mirrors in them, since a great many people are able to occupy themselves quite happily by looking at their reflection and doing things to their clothes or faces. The problem which to a non-lateral thinker would have been one of speed was solved laterally by making the time, not the lift, move more quickly.

De Bono does not say anything directly about careers in his book, but he does make a comment which is very relevant to the job-hunting process:

> Whenever units are assembled together and given a new
> name or label, this becomes so easily established that
> one tends to forget what lies underneath the label. By
> abolishing the label one can rediscover what there is
> underneath. One may find much use that was previously
> hidden. One may find there is very little of importance
> even though the label itself seemed important . . .
> de Bono, *Lateral Thinking* (Penguin)

The fact is that most people think of themselves in label
terms. They have been a sales manager, doing a certain set
of jobs, so they *are* a sales manager. They have been a
research chemist, so they aim for a job as a laboratory
head. This view of oneself can be enormously inhibiting
and may lead to someone moving from one job where they
have been unsuccessful and/or unhappy to another of the
same ilk. For this reason, career consultants devote a great
deal of time, right at the beginning of the counselling
process, to helping their clients discover what is under-
neath those labels. Apart from asking you to go over the
ground in your life cycle as well as your career cycle, as we
have done in the previous chapter, they get you to spend a
lot of time – as much as two or three weeks – before you
even start looking for a job in listing your achievements.
You are asked to think about the external circumstances in
which you produced them, the personal qualities which you
brought to bear on them and the constraints you had to
overcome on the way there. The career consultants,
Frederick Chusid, who are one of the firms who attach
great importance to this process, call it the 'unique ability
analysis'. You will find, when you have completed this
exercise, that certain patterns recur – what one writer
called Success Factors. These factors, once indentified, will
help you in two ways. Firstly, they will indicate the
ingredients of a job in which you would be likely to perform
successfully; secondly, they will help you strip off the
labels that are glued on to you by unjustified preconceptions and assumptions. This does not mean you can move
in some totally different direction, some career fantasy
unrelated to your past, but it may enable you to establish
that the label you have had on you is not quite the right
one: the mediocre systems analyst but excellent report
writer might be a potential technical author rather than a
computer specialist. Thirdly, it will help you enormously

with the compilation of your CV, which is probably the most important single document in your job search and which we will deal with in a later chapter.

Though it helps, obviously, to have professional help in the difficult task of self assessment – particularly since it is notoriously difficult to be objective about oneself – it is not indispensible. You can do a lot yourself with the help of an intelligent friend/companion/wife to take the place of the career counsellor's searching questions about how true and realistic your self image is.

Achievements

Listing your achievements has some therapeutic value which career counsellors consider important where people have been made redundant or are having difficulty finding a job, because when morale is low it is generally accompanied or preceded by self doubt. Looking at what you have done is an essential step to picking up the pieces that will build your future but, like a pile of bricks, they are not that meaningful lying about in isolation. What is significant is how they fit together. In the job context this means identifying which skills and attributes have played a part in your success. It is highly likely that they will form a recurring pattern which will indicate that you have certain gifts which contribute to every achievement you feel you have reached.

For instance, let us take the case of John Smith (for obvious reasons not a real name, though a real case history). John graduated with a BA honours in economics in 1962 and after a spell in the London Office of a well known chemical conglomerate, has since then been working in Africa. In 1982 he was getting increasingly concerned about his and his family's future there and asked for a job in the London headquarters. He had performed well and was considered, in fact, to be at the upper end of the middle management spectrum, though not destined for the top. His company felt that they already had too many people of John's calibre in London and were unable to offer him a post there.

John took a look at the high points in his career and this is what he came up with:

1965: While a marketing executive in the London office, where he started to work not long after graduating, he was sent out to Africa to examine dealership arrangements on behalf of the company's battery division. It was a three-month tour and at the end of it he wrote a report which recommended and gave some proposals for the implementation of changes which resulted in a 50 per cent increase in turnover over the subsequent two years. A pleasant by-product of this exercise was a considerable reduction in bad debts in the territory. For this, John was personally commended by the MD of the subsidiary company for whom he had prepared the report. The skills which had played a role in his success were collecting and analysing data, presenting them for action and, to some extent, problem solving.

1966–70: Area Manager, Malawi. He was responsible for all aspects of the company's activities and increased turnover by 60 per cent, firstly by pursuing a more aggressive policy towards obtaining government contracts and secondly by identifying new and hitherto unsuspected markets for various of his company's products. A highlight of his time in Malawi was when he was asked to serve on a government committee on the economic development of rural areas – a role which was also very useful from a business point of view. Ultimately, he achieved a successful handover of his job to a Malawi national. Once again, he was good in situations which involved analysing data and interpreting it into plans for action. He also developed skills in negotiating and, in the handover phase, in teaching and delegating.

1970–74: Managing Director, Tanzania. The achievement he was proudest of there was a barter arrangement which made it possible to get round Tanzania's very strict regulations on the transfer of funds out of the country. Otherwise it was very difficult to get much done because of the economic situation, though John did have some success in introducing a new insecticide which grabbed a substantial share of the market. What he enjoyed most, though, was his involvement in planning and building a new warehouse for the company's small distribution facility. Relating his gift for analytical problem solving to helping to create a building was a new skill he discovered, though he has been good at art while at school. Otherwise he had found his time in Tanzania somewhat frustrating.

1974–82: Marketing Director, South Africa. This was a

step up, though not a decisive one. Probably his most significant contribution during those years came about when he realised that there were a number of South African agrichemical products which were superior to those his company was marketing. He urged that they should acquire the licence to sell these in other markets and led the team that conducted the negotiations. Subsequently they were successfully introduced into Australia and a number of other territories. He also realised that his company was missing out in the market for domestic garden chemicals and launched a drive in that direction. By the time he left, that sector was accounting for over 20 per cent of annual profits in South Africa. By far his most enjoyable task, though, was when, because of his earlier experience, he was put in charge of working with the architects on re-planning and extending the firm's distribution facilities in Cape Town, Durban and Johannesburg.

Management texts tell us that doing any job, no matter what it is, involves carrying out certain courses of action and deploying certain skills and attributes. Their range is, in fact, surprisingly limited and can be narrowed down as follows:

- Managing, decision making
- Organising and administration
- Planning
- Controlling expenditure
- Creating and innovating, verbally or with objects
- Negotiating and persuading
- Collecting and analysing data
- Advising – presenting verbal or numerical data for action by others
- Problem solving
- Teaching and delegating
- Communicating

In John's case, his career suggests that he is good at collecting and analysing data and at presenting it for action by others. Planning, creating and innovating also feature strongly and he seems to have had some success as a negotiator. However, organising and administrating in the more abstract sense, controlling expenditure, 'being a manager', leading a sales force – none of these loom large in his career path. Perhaps he never had a chance to do them. More likely other things interested him more and if he is going to make a move he ought to be looking at opportunities that point in the direction of his success factors.

Anyone could do this exercise for themselves and even elaborate on it to establish a profile of the attributes and skills they brought into action at high points in their career. You don't need to be a 42-year-old executive either. A recent undergraduate who has organised a sports tour, or a band, done a vacation job, sat on a committee – made any sort of contribution to anything – could identify the job characteristics he was good at, and so could a school leaver.

Personal Characteristics

A fair amount of pseudo-science can be involved in identifying personal characteristics that make for success. Some of the more old-fashioned tests, for instance, come up with concepts like 'phlegmatic' or 'altruistic' personalities that are supposed to indicate various career paths. It all sounds slightly medieval. A brisker view of things was advanced by the nineteenth century Prussian general, von Moltke, who said all officers fell into only two categories – they were either clever or stupid. These qualities, he said, were invariably combined with one of two other attributes: lazy or industrious. Those who were clever and industrious were fitted for the most senior commands, while those who were clever but idle made good staff officers. Those who were stupid and industrious were good commanders at a lower level, whereas those who were both idle and stupid made up the general run of regimental officers.

This is a trifle simplistic – though not without an element of cruel truth – but the point is that even von Moltke, a man who one assumes would have had little patience with industrial psychology, acknowledges that personal characteristics play a very important role in success or failure. A virtue in one position may be a vice in another – an impulsive person, for instance, might be a square peg in a round hole as a planner – so there are few absolutes, but it is necessary to identify your characteristics in looking at what direction you ought to go in for the future.

In John Smith's case, one very positive aspect is his adaptability. He has shown this not only by making the move to Africa in the first place, but by the way he seems to have moved quite happily between the various cultural settings while he was there. Although Malawi, Tanzania and South Africa are all in sub-equatorial Africa, as societies they have little in common. Adaptability is a good characteristic to have when conditions are as unstable as they have been during the last decade, but there are many other characteristics which could have had a very considerable bearing on your success (or failure) in past jobs. They point to working environments you should seek – or keep away from – in the future. How could you class yourself on the following characteristics?

	Very	*Fairly*	*Neutral*	*Fairly*	*Very*	
Adaptable						Rigid
Warm						Aloof
Emotionally stable						Subject to ups and downs
Sociable						Loner
Easy going						Difficult
Quick to enthuse						Cautious
Self disciplined						Needs rules
Conscientious						Careless
Self confident						Insecure
Can judge own performance						Needs praise and approval
Easily taken in						Hard to fool
Determined						Easily discouraged
Imaginative						Unimaginative
Practical						Impractical
Impulsive						Deliberate
Decisive						Indecisive
Realistic						A dreamer
Tolerant						Critical
Tactful						Tactless
Talkative						Discreet
Sensitive						Insensitive
Prepared to take critisism						Touchy
Punctual						Unpunctual
Popular						Unpopular
Outgoing						Inhibited
Resourceful						Passive
Assertive						Timid

It is possible to go on extending this list, but these characteristics probably cover the main ones that are relevant to most types of work. In one guise or another they are used in quite a number of tests and it is of course possible to criticise them as being 'it depends on the situation' attributes. One might, for instance, be quite resourceful in solving an intellectual problem, but hopeless in dealing with a burst water main. Overall though, *and in relation to a practical job objective*, you will find some useful self-assessment guidance by rating yourself on some such scale as this.

External Factors

Achievements, and what brought them about, are not, of course, solely conditioned by the attributes and personal characteristics that you brought to bear on them. External factors will also have played a part, though there may well be points of contact between various elements of the situation; because of the way you are, you may respond to the carrot or to the stick, or indeed to particular kinds of carrot or stick. For instance, the need to seek praise or approval clearly relates to status which, apart from money and job satisfaction is one of the top three attributes most people would regard as important. Here are some others which will probably have contributed to a sense of achievement:

- A compatible working group in terms of personalities, size or complementary skills
- Dealing with people you liked, inside and outside the organisation
- A compatible organisation
- Variety of work
- The right amount of responsibility
- Security
- A good physical environment to work in
- An agreeable part of the world
- The right amount of pressure
- Access to as much staff and equipment as you needed to do the job

Again, this is not a finite list – you can make up your own list of those factors which you feel have led to a sense of success in the past and which you ought to look for in your next job.

Dream Jobs

As part of the self-analysis and self-assessment procedure, many counselling firms ask their clients to describe what their dream job would be like. Some American firms, in fact, carry this exercise to great lengths, even asking their clients to describe in minute detail the appearance of the workplace, the people they see themselves working with and so forth.

Without taking it to extremes there are a number of reasons why formulating a dream job can be valuable. One of them is to get it out of your system, but in a healthy and constructive way. Retreating into agreeable fantasies about the infinite possibilities open to them now that they have shed corporate ties can be one of those temporarily euphoric psychological states people looking for a job get into – only to plunge into depression when they come up against reality and when the money starts to run out. So they are asked, in effect, to get it out of their system by listing all the things they would like to do.

What comes out is often rather strange. At the London Business School, for instance, it has been found that a lot of people want to be doctors, irrespective of their lack of medical qualifications and of the fact that medical training takes six years. Farming is also high on the list and so is running your own business, but with no specific type of business in mind – just the desire to be independent. For younger people the dream job is often to drop out of the orthodox job world altogether – to sail a boat round the Mediterranean, become a ski instructor or engage in some other activity where you get paid enough to live on for doing something you enjoy a lot. Also popular is the wish to re-train in a new kind of job, usually related to leisure pursuits that have become more attractive than the actual job you were doing: photography, perhaps, or becoming a teacher in a subject that interests you. Finally, there may be aspects of your present and previous jobs that you found rewarding out of all proportion to anything else you did in it. John Smith, for instance, has become very seriously interested in architecture as a result of his involvement with planning warehouses for his company.

In this 'dream job' exercise, people are asked to say why they have chosen it, what their role would be called, what qualifications and training it would need, what you expect to earn, where you would be doing it, what hours you would be working; and, of course, how it relates to the mix of job and personal characteristics as well as to the external factors that contributed to your previous achievements.

By this time the contact between reality and fantasy may be getting uncomfortably close, but there is more to come, because you are asked to list all the things which you think will prevent you from doing or getting your dream job. John Smith, for instance, found that his creative gift for problem solving, his extensive business experience and his never-used A level in art did seem to point to the fact that he might 'make a go' of architecture. But standing in the way was the very long period of training involved, his lack of resources to keep his family during this time and ultimately the diminished opportunities in the profession itself. On the other hand he also felt – and he has a good record for sizing up opportunities – that with distribution of goods changing under the impact of new technology, if he specialised in that particular aspect he might eventually do quite well. The gap between fantasy and reality was capable of being closed, *if* he could solve the financial problems that it entailed and *if* he was willing to accept the fact that he was probably unlikely to recover his present earning power for years to come – assuming, that is, that he could find another marketing job.

That was one particular case and the constraints that stand in the way of your dream job vary from person to person. They can be lack of qualifications, too little money in the job, not enough money to invest, too old to start again, to young to start at all and so forth. Some are capable of being overcome and your chart of personal characteristics might indicate which these are; for instance, if you score poorly on self discipline you may not be successful at running your own business, however highly you rate on enthusiasm.

The object of this exercise is not, however, to pour cold water on your waking dreams. Like the ones you have while asleep, they are significant. In the first place it may be perfectly possible to reach them, provided you are aware of the obstacles in your way, have the determination and have or can get the means – whatever they may be – to overcome them. Secondly, they indicate what you really want to do. It may not be possible to do exactly that, but perhaps there are jobs that have *some* of the ingredients you value. For instance, becoming a farmer may be a

practical impossibilty, but what is feasible is a job in a
rural area, perhaps at a lower salary, where you can run
some sort of smallholding in your spare time. Furthermore,
what you want to do is almost certainly what you would be
good at doing and may therefore point in some general
career direction. The industrial chemist who wants to be
an author may be nourishing an impossible dream if he
wants to become another C P Snow – a research chemist
who became a highly successful novelist – but he or she
should certainly be looking seriously at prospects for
technical writers.

Thirdly, and rather brutally, it may destroy some fantasies altogether, but this is no bad thing if they bear no
relation to reality. Though it is not as bad as dwelling
obsessively on the past, career counsellors do not encourage fantasising about the future. By definition, fantasies
are unattainable, even in better job markets then the
present ones.

Employees and Entrepreneurs

Arising out of these various self-assessment exercises,
some very interesting broad career conclusions have been
reached by Dr Ronnie Lessem, Director of the Urban
Economic Development Group (URBED) which, among
other activities, runs courses for intending entrepreneurs.
There are some people, he has found, whose success factors
clearly do not point towards an independent entrepreneurial role. Such people tend to be good at designing and
running activities but not at taking the initiative and
responding to emerging needs.

When such executives are made redundant, they find it
easier to take over an existing franchise or business than
to start a new one. They also like creating business plans
or blueprints because they want to structure their world.
It is this very need for structure which prevents them
from entering into the unknown.

The sort of people who are happier and more likely to
make a success of self-employment in present and emerging economic conditions are firstly what he calls 'enab-
lers'. These are people who see 'patterns and connections
between people and between products and markets ...
Rather than creating new enterprises from scratch, they

enhance existing ones through making physical, human and financial connections and participating in the result.' That kind of person, in practical terms, would be someone with a substantial golden handshake who would use it to take over an existing business and set it off in new directions which the previous owners have missed because they have not been able to look beyond the 'labels' of their preconceptions.

The second kind of person who Dr Lessem believes will make a success of self-employment is the extraverted, outward-going and opportunistic entrepreneur. That person, he believes, will grasp the points we have made in Chapter 2 about the changing nature of work and employment. For instance, he points to the fact that one of Britain's most dynamic companies, Sinclair Electronics, only 'employs' about forty people and subcontracts most of its work out. 'With the "Office of the Future",' Dr Lessem says. 'This trend is bound to be accelerated.' The fact that words like 'extraverted, outward-going and opportunistic' could be applied to Sir Freddie Laker as well as Clive Sinclair points however to the fact that to be a successful entrepreneur you need a lot of very down-to-earth qualities as well as vision, flair and imagination.

Professional Career Analysis

If you feel completely at sea about the next step in your career or if you feel you cannot see any kind of pattern in the events that have so far determined its course – or simply if you are still too young for such a pattern to have developed – you would probably be well-advised to seek professional help. Some kind of formal psychological appraisal is usually included in the process of career counselling with which we will deal in Chapter 8, but it is also possible to get such an appraisal done as a separate exercise. Possibly the best known firm in the field are *Career Analysts* (90 Gloucester Place, London W1), who provide career guidance, based on testing, for people of all ages between 15 and 54. They charge between £80 –£100 for a one-day session.

The contents and nature of the tests which are administered obviously vary according to your age group, but the methods and aims are broadly similar. Before the actual consultation you are asked to complete a personal data form. This gives a picture of your educational and career progress to date and is designed in such a way as to show how it relates to your personality, attitudes and ambitions – as expressed, for instance, in what you choose to do in your spare time.

Then come the actual tests themselves. These are established psychological tests, your answers to which identify interests under the headings of scientific, welfare, persuasive, literary, artistic, computational and practical. When these interests are set alongside the results of a further test dealing with aptitudes, such as the ability to reason in a verbal, numerical, mechanical or spatial terms, some career indications begin to emerge. For instance, an artistic range of interests combined with an aptitude for understanding spatial relationships would point to a design-oriented career.

A further written test then examines personal characteristics and constraints. These indicate the level of work and the type of organisation you would be happiest with in the light of what your previous responses have already shown. Finally, there is an interview with a consultant at which all the findings are discussed and specific suggestions are made about the practical steps you should take to implement any new career directions the tests have suggested. All this is then embodied in a written report which they send you.

Services of this kind are criticised in some quarters as being, potentially, exercises in shutting the stable door after the horse has bolted. It is very little use, for instance, telling a middle-aged marketing man that he would have done much better in the legal profession, and cases like this have apparently occurred where advice has been sought from some of the less practical and established firms administering tests of this kind. Furthermore, evidence of aptitude and interest in a certain area is not in itself sufficient to get a job in it. Your tests may indicate that you have enormous potential ability as an advertising copywriter, for instance, but you would still find it very difficult to get a job in an agency without previous experience. The younger you are, obviously, and the fewer commitments you have, the more it is possible to re-train yourself on the lines suggested in your career analysis. For older people, its chief value is that it provides an independent compass reading for the general direction your job search should take – or not take, as the case may be. This is very valuable from a morale as well as a more immediately practical point of view. Provided you are clear about its limitations, professional career analysis based on test procedures could well be worth its rather reasonable cost.

6. Organising Your Resources

The preparations for conducting a job search or a change in career patterns that we have been talking about so far have mainly been rather general, though very necessary ones – looking at the employment scene as a whole, at what the criteria are for making a move and at what sort of move might be indicated by your personality, achievements, characteristics and aims.

One option resulting from such a survey might be to re-evaluate your attitudes to work and employment; to decide not to compete in the orthodox job market at all, but to look more closely at the range of 'Alternatives' discussed in the last three chapters of this book.

There is some evidence that the Americans are more ready than we have been so far to recognise in terms of alternatives, the implications of the shrinking market in traditional jobs. A young British executive, living quite happily as an odd-job man in Aspen, Colorado, told a *Guardian* interviewer in September 1982:

> What it boils down to is attitude. We don't have careers any more. Being something or other – we're not that. Therefore we're free to do anything. I might clean out garbage dumpsters this winter or shovel snow. I don't know and it doesn't worry me. I couldn't go back and mow lawns in England, could I? Firstly I couldn't live on it, and besides there's all that social stigma.

Dropping out? Not really, because this young man is not drifting, he has merely reorganised his life in a new way. If that is what you are thinking of doing you should go on a TOPS or YOPS course, because the real value of such courses is probably much more that they are a passport to skills that can be used in the new world of work envisaged by people like Alvin Toffler or Dr Lessem:

> Moonlighting, management buy-outs, franchising, part-time employment, freelance work, sub-contracting, autonomous profit centres, new ventures, co-operatives, new businesses, work sharing, consultancy; all of these are alternatives.
>
> (*Industrial and Commercial Training,* October 1982)

YOPS and TOPS would be a lot more use if they were more fully and perhaps even formally, established as a staging post in this kind of economy, backed up by advice and – much more useful than indiscriminate financial aid – start-up contracts from local authorities – than the dead end they turn out, more often than not, to be in terms of orthodox jobs.

But what about the executive in mid-career who feels he or she is not cut out for self-employment and who just wants another job? It is no use pretending that their task will be an easy one, but there are ways in which it can be made lighter. One of the main problems of the job search, it has often been noted, is that people begin with high hopes, and as disappointments pile up and the money runs out, demoralisation sets in – sometimes to the extent that they end up being virtually unemployable. The best way to avoid this syndrome is to set yourself realistic targets, based on properly organised research into the job market, and related to your resources. That way you can, at least to some extent, control the situation, instead of being, as so many people feel they are, utterly at the mercy of events.

How Long Will It Take?

In making plans for an uncertain future, the question obviously arises of how long it will take you to find a job. One factor here is age. It has to be said that over 50 it gets progressively harder. At the other extreme, an article in the *Sunday Times* stated that in 1981 'as many as about one in eight of Britain's graduates had still not found permanent work – of any kind – six months after taking their degree'. This is bad, but it still means that seven out of eight graduates do get jobs fairly quickly, though the competition for them is intense and there is evidence of a downward drift in their status: graduates are applying for jobs that used to go to 18-year-olds with A levels, and A level school leavers are looking around for what used to be post-O level jobs.

No figures are available for the proportion of over-fifties who are able to find another job, but since every career counsellor (we will deal with their role in Chapter 8) claims a high success rate – some as much as 100 per cent – and since quite a number of their clients are in their fifties, it is clearly not a mission impossible. For instance, a privately issued survey produced by the career counsellors Forty Plus shows that in the first six months of 1982 they placed twenty-two people in jobs at between £10,000 and £40,000 a year (the average was around £20,000). The majority were on the 'wrong' side of 45 and several were in their fifties, yet out of the twenty-two, eighteen were placed within six months. The best opportunities seem to turn up in smaller companies. Past the age of 55, though, career counsellors do often urge people who come to them for advice to think of early retirement, self-employment, temporary work or voluntary posts rather than trying to get back on to the employed job market.

Those, of any age, with a record of undue job hopping may also find things difficult. Too many jobs with different organisations in too short a space of time, unfortunately, is a frequent cause for being eliminated before the interview stage. Recruiters take the view that you need about two years to make any impact on a job – a point that anyone considering a voluntary move ought to take into account.

Given, though, that you do fall into the age group of the majority of the working population – between 25 and 48 – and have had a reasonably consistent job record, consultants suggest a rule of thumb for the length of the job search: four months for the first £10,000 of the target salary and a month for every £1,500 above that. Like all rules of thumb, of course, these are subject to considerable variations – the highly qualified technologist in a growth area in his or her thirties is not likely to take ten months to find a £20,000 job if they have any idea of how to market themselves properly. Tom Carew of Percy Coutts Ltd. claims that with good advice on that point he can cut the waiting time by about 50 per cent and quite a number of career counsellors say that they reckon to place most of their clients within six months.

What is unlikely, though, is that you will find a job

immediately, and in neglecting this simple point some people rule themselves out almost from the start. In the panic phase of their search they write off letters and applications to all and sundry without sufficient consideration of their ability to meet the job specification; or in the case of 'on spec' approaches (a subject we will deal with in more detail later) without the very careful preparation that this requires. When only 6–10 applicants out of ten times that number are even called for interview, there is very little chance that such long shots will find their target. In most cases it is this kind of random way of going about it that is behind the horror stories one reads of people applying for literally hundreds of jobs without getting a single interview. The fact is, furthermore, that such indiscriminate approaches are self-defeating. One recruitment consultant said – and the story was confirmed by others – that:

> In these days when everything is computerised, the big recruitment consultants have records of people who consistently apply for jobs and get turned down. If a name keeps on recurring and getting rejected at the interview or even before, the tendency is to write them off as a loser and eventually simply not to forward their name to the client . . . If you're consistently failing to get an interview, you're either applying for the wrong jobs, or there's something seriously wrong with your CV or letter application.

The Job of Looking for a Job

How much time should you allot to the job search? Some career consultants maintain that it should be a full-time occupation, but to some extent this may be because they find that people, after a while, slip all too easily into a routine of demoralised inactivity. Clearly, devoting all one's time to job hunting is not a practicable proposition for everybody. Some people may need or want to take up temporary or part-time jobs, a matter dealt with in Chapter 13. Others, particularly those with working wives (or parents or husbands) would feel under some obligation to take on a bigger share in the household chores than they used to do; or there may simply be jobs around the house that they have been putting off doing for years and that they now have time for. Nothing wrong with that – that is

63

work too. Even if you do not get paid for it, you save money by not having to pay someone else to do it. The important thing is to allocate a regular day, or a regular part of the day, to matters connected with the job serach.

To some extent these may be determined by when the most job ads appear. Obviously the quality Sundays are an important source and so are papers that carry specially heavy job advertisement pages at certain days of the week – the Thursday *Daily Telegraph*, for instance. Then there are days when there is a specialist section of job ads: media jobs appear once a week in the *Guardian* and there is a day for legal jobs in the *Financial Times*, to give just two examples. Going beyond that, there are specialist, professional and trade papers, while for junior and middle management the local press is becoming increasingly attractive for employers because of the horrendous cost of national advertising. All this is apart from the biggest single source of job ads, the freesheet *Executive Post* which goes out to everyone on the PER register and lists about 400 jobs every week, mostly in middle and supervisory management. It now also has a stablemate called *Graduate Post*, which contains details of jobs and courses for those who are about to graduate or who have recently done so. The reason why it is important to coincide one's maximum effort on days when job ads are concentrated is because these days you have to react quickly. If, by the time you have put together your letter and CV a fortnight has elapsed, it is highly likely that the recruiter has already made up his or her mind about whom they want to see from the applications that are already in.

Keeping an eye on all this information could be an expensive exercise – the newsagent's bills alone could make a large hole in the weekly budget. A very sensible economy, therefore, is to use your local reference library, because although book budgets have been cut back, as publishers have found to their cost, few of the periodicals and papers you are likely to need have been cancelled.

They are worth looking at not only for their direct job content, but also for the peripheral information. We shall show in the chapter on the unadvertised job market what an immensely valuable source of job leads this can be, but it also has considerable importance simply in terms of keeping up with your subject. It is very easy to get out of touch very quickly with news, views and technical information in your field – which you will need to have at your fingertips in interviews. The larger libraries will also have reference sections containing books which pinpoint information on specific companies that are advertising jobs or to whom you might be thinking of making an 'on spec' approach. Some of the leading sources are:

- *UK Kompass Register*: An annual two-volume publication which provides basic information on the location, staffing, activities, products and services of thousands of companies.

- *Dun & Bradstreets's Guide to Key British Enterprises*: Gives details of anything that might be described as a major company, including activities, sales turnover and names of directors.

- *Dun & Bradstreet's British Middle Market Directory*: Provides similar information on medium sized companies.

- *Who Owns Whom*: Also published by Dun & Bradstreet, this book, as the name implies, discloses relationships between companies and their subsidiaries.

- *The Times 1,000 Leading Companies*: An annual publication giving details of the performance and activities of the 1,000 largest UK companies.

- *The Journal of Executive Recruitment*: A relatively new monthly journal which, in addition to some useful editorial, claims to contain many jobs not advertised elsewhere.

- *Who's Who*: If you are writing to someone prominent, this annual publication lists all sorts of personal information about them that might be useful in an interview.

- *British Qualifications*: If someone you want to see has a string of peculiar letters after his or her name, this tells you what they mean.

- *Stock Exchange Yearbook*: Another source of financial information on all quoted public companies.

- *Extel Cards*: A bible for stock exchange punters, these cards cover the performance and activities of both quoted and unquoted companies.

- *Executive Grapevine*: A useful directory of headhunters

and their specialisations. Now unfortunately out of print but you may get it from your library.
- There are also a number of career directories aimed at recent or prospective graduates: *Graduate Opportunities* (GO), *Directory of Opportunities for Graduates* (GET) and several others. Some of these are of limited value to job seekers and seem to be published largely in order to sell advertising space.

One source of background information career counsellors advise people to use as little as possible if they are out of a job is their old workplace. Indeed, an important aspect of their initial task with people who go to them for help is to get them to break the 'umbilical cord' with their previous firm. Jim Smith of MSL speaks for many of his colleagues in saying:

My first task is to get people to 'disidentify' with the organisation they worked for before. They've got to learn to detach themselves from the past and start thinking about the future.

The trouble is that after years with a firm – and one does after all spend more time at work than in any other activity or relationship – one can get so involved with it and the people in it that it is a real wrench to break away completely, especially when the parting has been an amicable one. The temptation to slip back to the old office and linger there under the pretext of getting information should be resisted as much as possible. Whatever expressions of regret there may have been at your departure, 'the dogs bark, the caravan moves on'.

Financial Aspects

To some extent the course of your job search will be dictated by how long you can stretch out your financial resources. Piers Wemyss of PA Consultants has some sensible rule of thumb advice on this point:

You've got to accept that it will take time. The most sensible way to approach it is to look at your liquid resources and assets and decide how long they will last you. Then divide your search period into three sub-periods. In the first third, look for a better job. In the second third, look for a sideways move. Finally, be prepared to take anything reasonable to tide you over – and try to move upwards again as soon as you can.

There are, of course, ways in which one's resources can be spun out over a long period of time. You can scrimp and save. One otherwise sensible book on surviving redundancy has suggestions like using two buttons linked with a piece of thread to replace cuff links or making one tea bag last for two pots – but the question you have to ask yourself is what such measures will do to your morale and that of those around you. Most counsellors in fact advise that you should live as close to your normal standard as possible, for as long as possible, merely cutting out really unnecessary luxuries (like taxis or expensive wines) for the time being. Certainly you should be very wary of cutting back social activities, not only because of the psychological dangers of isolating yourself, but because friends and acquaintances can be an invaluable source of job leads. Even abandoning a planned holiday is not necessarily a good idea. A lot of interviewers are guided by first impressions and in such cases applicants who look fit and healthy generally stand a better chance.

It is only in the second and third phases of your search that you should consider serious applications of the surgeon's knife to your domestic economy, and then it is a matter of sitting down with your family, if you have one, and deciding what it would hurt everyone least to do without. In no case, though, should you dispense with anything that materially affects your appearance – shabby clothes and down-at-heel shoes are a very false economy indeed; and if you are in the habit of taking a daily swim or playing a weekly round of golf, try to keep it up. Numerous doctors have testified to the increased health hazards facing those out of work.

If You Are in A Job

If you are in a job, looking for one is much easier in some ways (financial ones, for instance), much more difficult in others. It is easier in the sense that although what used, frankly, to be prejudice against people who have been made redundant has diminished enormously because so many are in that position, the person still in a job has the

edge in a competitive situation where all else is equal. For
this reason, Hugh Roc of Chubbs, as well as many other
people in personnel and recruitment, think it is a good idea
to take on temporary work, especially if you have had a
longish spell of unemployment. The longer you have exceeded the 'normal' period out of a job, the more difficult it
becomes to find another one. Taking on temporary work,
provided it is reasonably appropriate, is, Hugh Roc says:

A good sign. For one thing it means that the person is
resourceful. It also means they're keeping their hand in
with working – it's all too easy to drift out of the work
habit. But most of all it means they're adaptable and can
muck in. A lot of the opportunities now are in smaller
firms and there's always a fear there that someone might
be too grand for some of the more tedious aspects of
executive jobs; particularly, again, in small firms where
you tend to have to turn your hand to anything at times.

The difficult aspect in this situation, or if you are still in
your job, is that all your research into general and specific
opportunities, and the whole business of writing letters
and compiling CVs has to be done in the evenings and at
weekends. There is also the problem of getting away for
interviews. If your employer knows you are looking for a
job, he will not normally object to your going off for an
occasional interview – certainly if you have been made
redundant he or she is obliged to give you reasonable time
off for this purpose. The situation is obviously more complicated if they are in blissful ignorance, and if you wish them
to remain so you will have to try and fix interviews after
work. A prospective employer who is really interested in
you will not object to staying late to see you – on the
contrary it may well be a point in your favour that you are
doing your job hunting in your time rather than that of
your present employers.

There is, however, a danger in conducting prolonged
'fishing expeditions'. At some point your present employer
is going to get to hear about it – particularly if you are
working in a small, tightly-knit industry like one of the
media. Their reaction will then be in one of two directions.
They will either offer you more money to stay or they too
will start looking around for someone to replace you. 'At
some point you really have to make the decision to go or

stay,' says Genie Hart of Minister Executive. 'You can't put out a lot of feelers without someone getting to hear about it and it's usually the one person you'd rather didn't know.'

Organising Your Records

In these days when a job search takes months rather than weeks and you have to apply for at least ten jobs to get even one interview, it is all too easy to get into a mess on the paperwork side. For this reason job counsellors advise keeping proper files. One suggested method is to have a central file containing items like your National Insurance certificates and P45, documentation of any qualifications, the master CV which you will adapt to the circumstances of any particular job, the results of any tests you have taken and any material from which you compiled the CV, even if it is something for your personal use only.

Then you should have a record of every job you have applied for – the advertisement itself, copies of letters, any literature about the employer, whether it is stuff you compiled yourself or his own handouts. This obviously needs to be studied closely before you attend an interview; and should you get to that stage, you should make a record of who you saw and what transpired – particularly any mistakes in your technique or questions that floored you, so that you can get it right next time.

You should also keep two diaries, one to carry with you and one to keep beside the telephone, so that if anyone phones while you are out appointments schedules can be checked by whoever picks up the call. A good investment, if you live alone or if the house is likely to be empty during the day, is an answerphone. These efficient little devices can now be bought for under £100 and if that seems like a lot of money, compare it to the salary you are after.

One reason why it is important to keep these records is that because of the weight of applications that are often received when a tempting job is advertised it may take weeks before someone contacts you. If you have several irons in the fire simultaneously, which is what you should be doing no matter how promising one particular avenue looks, it is all too easy to get jobs mixed up when the call comes through. As they used to say in one of the whisky ads, 'don't say "who", say "when"'. The best way to get into that position is to have your information field organised in a way that at least you can understand.

7. Putting Yourself Across: How to Write CVs That Get Interviews

Whether your job search is a full-time occupation or not, there is one aspect of it to which you will have to devote a great deal of time and attention: compiling your CV. You need a CV to work from even if the job advertisement requires you to fill in an application form or even if you are a skilful enough writer to weave your career details into a letter of application which incorporates a CV. In any case, if you look at job advertisements you will see that the vast majority of them ask for a CV in the first instance. It is, in the apt phrase used by one of the companies that advertises professionally prepared CVs, 'your first interview'. The growing number of firms offering such services indicates that many job seekers find this an alarming prospect.

The are certainly right to take it seriously. In present employment conditions, those engaged in recruitment at any level report that for any remotely desirable job that is not too highly specialised, 80 – 100 applications are usual, around 200 not uncommon and there have been instances where as many as 1,000 applications are received. Only one person can be chosen and not many are called for interview: twenty at most and usually not more than ten. Put yourself in the place of the person who is processing the application and try to think how you can get over his or her boredom and impatience threshold, especially if it is around lunchtime. 'Some applicants eliminate themselves right away,' says Michael Armstrong, author of several standard texts on personnel management and himself personnel director of Book Club Associates. "Ill written, badly arranged, mis-spelled, discursive or boastful CVs barely get looked at, particularly if they're handwritten as well.'

These may sound like fairly obvious guidelines, except that a great many younger job seekers seem to ignore them. But if a tendency to scruffiness is a fault of youth and inexperience, the fault of their elders is to go on about things at wearisome length. Most consultants seem to agree that a CV should be no more than three pages long at the outside and probably not more than two. Anything longer than that is almost bound to contain irrelevancies and the person who is processing upwards of 100 applications – and therefore reading at least 200 pages of type-script – simply will not stop to sift the nuggets of gold from anything resembling a sackful of sand.

Quite a lot can be achieved simply by creating a good first impression. 'A lot of CVs come as badly folded bits of paper,' says John Fuller of Personal CV, one of the professional CV writers. 'You can get a small advantage by putting yours in a big envelope with a piece of board to keep it stiff. Not a gimmick, but it will stand out from most of the others.' Fuller also has an interesting tip on the follow-up. He says, "It's a good idea to phone a few days after sending your CV off. It creates a contact with someone in the sifting and screening process. It may be someone inportant. For a few seconds at least, your name will be in his or her mind. If your CV has already been consigned to the reject list, maybe they'll take another look at it.'

Apart from the visual aspects of presentation – neat lay-out, good typing on white paper, information arranged so that its salient points are easy to take in at first glance – there are also the actual contents. The basics are:

- Name
- Address
- Telephone number
- Date of Birth
- Marital status
- Education and qualifications
- Career history in reverse chronological order, beginning with the most recent job and concentrating on the last ten years. Earlier periods can be summarised as 'early career' to keep the CV down to a maximum length of three pages. Where the CV is being sent as

part of an 'on spec' approach (ie without your having a particular post in mind) there should be a brief note about what sort of job you are looking for, in what sort of company and what your aims, ambitions and qualifications are – see Chapter 10, *Inside the Unadvertised Job Market*.

These are the bare bones that are recommended in many of the textbooks and the middle third of applicants – that is, those who don't fall at the first hurdle – consider them enough. Sadly, in today's highly competitive job market it is not usually enough just to get the basics right. That is why many applicants after weeks or even months of failing to get interviews, turn to professional CV writers.

The Professionally Written CV

The CV writers who advertise their services in the recruitment pages will send you a form in which you are asked to set out the details of your career, qualifications and achievements in a lot of detail. From this information a skilled copywriter will produce a professionally prepared CV, properly laid out on good paper (ask to see a sample of their work if they are not one of the well-known firms). It costs about £60 and they will run off extra copies at a modest additional charge.

There used to be quite a lot of prejudice against the manufactured CV but this seems to have lessened as more and more people are using them. Piers Wemyss reckons that a high proportion of the CVs he gets have been produced with professional help. 'How I view that depends somewhat on the job the person is applying for. If it's a post as an air traffic controller in Saudi Arabia, I'd assume that the ability to communicate in writing isn't very important. On the other hand where the job called for the ability to analyse data and present its salient points in written form – in fact the sort of skill involved in producing a CV – I'd probably feel that that person wasn't suitable.' The fact of the matter is that an experienced recruiter can tell a manufactured CV a mile off and it is not because it just looks slicker and more professional – there is nothing wrong with that – but because the information in it, though clearly presented and well laid out, is often not as totally relevant to the job in hand as the appearance of the document might at first make one think. This is really the snag of the professionally prepared CV.

The way to get round it is to write a letter every time you send out a 'portmanteau' CV (even if you have produced it yourself to meet all occasions), pointing out the features in it that relate to the particular job you are applying for. That at least shows you are not sending out a kind of round robin to every suitable job that come along, but have thought about the requirements of the job individually in the way we will suggest in the next chapter. This is more than just matter of courtesy to the person who has to read your CV. 'You've got to put over the *relevance* of your qualifications and experience right away,' says Michael Armstrong. 'And if you don't meet the job specification, you've got to produce a convincing and succinct reason why you should be called for an interview.'

Piers Wemyss underlines this remark:

> The information in your CV must be weighted to the needs of the job in question. If you're applying for a job as a senior project engineer to a firm supplying plant and equipment – a job which requires you to negotiate with clients and prepare tenders – you would want to highlight your experience in those spheres and not give equal weight to your work in less relevant fields; or, if you're applying for a job in marketing, but started your career as a designer you wouldn't want to go into enormous detail about that part of it – you'd merely want to show how design is relevant to marketing in that particular post.

The advice that emerges from all this is: if you are not confident enough of your skill in this department, use a professional CV writer by all means, but do not regard the document he produces as definitive for every occasion. Either use it as a model from which to compile CVs that are individually tailored to the job for which you are applying, or back it up with a job-specific letter. The fact is that no two jobs are exactly the same and if only 10 per cent of all applicants are called for interview, your chance of being rejected on marginal points of relevance are very great indeed.

Preparing Your Own CV

But supposing you want to prepare your own CV – and probably the majority of people still do – what tips can you pick up from the professionals who make a living at it? Here is a CV from an applicant who, though quite highly qualified, has very little idea of how to put over his story. His approach is typical of many CVs received every day by personnel directors and recruitment consultants.

PERSONAL DETAILS

Name: THOMAS LAWRENCE   Date of Birth: 4.2.43
Address: 3 Raeburn Road   Height: 5′ 10″
      Marchbourne   Weight: 13.12
      Hants XP3 2TT   Married: 2 children
Telephone: Marchbourne 1234

EDUCATION

Bishop Sedley Grammar   11 GCE 'O' level
School, Todhampton   3 GCE 'A' levels:
                              Physics, Maths, Music
Imperial College, London   BSc (Hons) Electronic
University   Engineering

WORK EXPERIENCE

1980– to date
Parkin & Stone Engineering Ltd: Management Systems Engineer responsible for system design, procurement and operator training in computer systems management for petrochemical plant and related equipment being supplied on a turnkey basis to overseas customers. Salary £18,000.

1977–80
Delphic Software Systems Ltd: Managing director (own business).

1972–70
Engineering Component Industries Ltd: Systems development engineer with special responsibility for automated machine processes. Before that, executive assistant to managing director.

1967–70
Southern Radio Industries Ltd: Production engineer. Trainee production engineer.

INTERESTS
Sailing
Music
Writing software programs for computer games

SPECIAL QUALIFICATIONS
Knowledge and practical experience of using Fortran, Algol, PL/1, Cobol, Basic as well as a number of less widely used machine codes. Developed, while at Engineering Component Industries, the software program, ARMREST.

Thomas Lawrence has had an interesting career and since he is in a 'hot' occupational field he stands a good chance of being called for an interview if there are not too many other applicants. The reason why one cannot rate it any higher is that his CV really tells you remarkably little, though it does raise a number of intriguing questions. What happened to his own business which he ran for three years? What exactly did he do in his other jobs, because he provides little more than lists of 'labels'. What is 'ARMREST'? A fellow engineer might know, but probably not a recruitment consultant. And what exactly does he mean when he says he 'developed' it? At the same time he tells the reader a number of things that are really of no interest to him. Why would he want to know his height and weight? At the most, the state of his general health might be of some value. Why disclose his salary? Most professional recruitment consultants advise against doing this unless you have to because it immediately limits your negotiating options.

How then would a professional CV writer present Lawrence's case? On the principle of the Irishman who, when asked for some directions, said that if that was where the stranger wanted to go he should not have gone that way at all, let us begin by looking at what a CV is *for*; unpeeling the label, in other words. Piers Wemyss sums up the general opinion of consultants and recruiters in saying that its aim is to arouse curiosity – to make the person reading it say, 'Ah yes, here's someone we need to see.' One of the leading American texts on personnel management says that, in order to do this, the CV (called a resumé in the States) should concentrate on the following aspects in every job the applicant has held:

- Profits: What impact did you have?
- Sales: What part did you play in increasing them?
- Costs: How were you able to reduce them in whatever sphere you worked?
- New Markets: What role did you play in developing them, with what impact on sales and profits, by product and/or by geographical area?
- Productivity: How did you increase it, by what means?
- Innovation: What did you do that was new? With what results on sales, profits, productivity?
- Job Function: How did you change it to enhance its contribution?
- Career plateaux: If you were apparently standing still, how did you increase the range of your responsibilities during this time?

So the first function of the CV is to arouse curiosity by implying that you can make a contribution to the job being advertised by demonstrating that you did so in your previous posts.

Secondly, you need to show that you are a problem solver. Most vacancies create problems or are the result of problems having appeared, as the best-selling American text on job-hunting, *What Color Is Your Parachute* points out. The two questions in any employer's mind are: will the new person be as good as the last incumbent? Or, will he or she be an improvement? 'Employers are worried about selection,' says Hugh Roc of Chubb's. 'They're afraid of making a mistake.' They want to get it right, because the costs of getting it wrong, taking all the factors into account, is never less than a full year's salary for the job and may be a lot more in the case of an absolute disaster. Ultimately their own judgment, even their own position, is at stake. So what they are looking for in the CV is some reassurance that they are going to get a problem solver, not a problem creator.

The third objective of the CV is to relate the self-assessment, self-analysis exercise we covered in the previous chapter to specific job opportunities – to review and focus your achievements, characteristics and constraints, put them in order and, in short, market them. By no means easy, but it is definitely worth the trouble if you look at what is at stake, even in terms of only one year's salary in your next job. This is why all career counsellors attach great importance to having their clients spend a great deal of time working at their CVs and the raw material that goes into it, as one of the first stages of consultation process.

On the other hand it is also important not to say too much. 'You've got to intrigue the reader,' says Piers Wemyss. 'If you tell him too much you become an open and shut case. That's not necessarily a good thing.' The way to do this initially is to present him or her with a good caption, rather in the way a newspaper headline is the first impulse towards making one want to read on. This, in John Lawrence's case, might be the following:

PROFILE

An industrial engineer/systems analyst, with experience across a wide spectrum of managerial and technological skills. Achievements include: Systems design and management in most advanced forms of petrochemical plant ● Design and installation of industrial robots ● Leading role in development of software programs for automated industrial processes ● Contract negotiations at government level ● Knowledge and practical experience of using an unusually wide range of main frame and microcomputer machine codes.

This would come immediately after PERSONAL DETAILS (confined to name, address, telephone number, date of birth, general health and marital status) and would be varied by highlighting any aspect that was particularly relevant to the post being advertised. The 'labels' in Lawrence's present CV would be amplified with a lot more information about what was behind them. For instance, under WORK EXPERIENCE:

1980 – to date
Parkin & Stone Engineering Ltd: Management Systems Engineer. Member of a five-man design team providing all systems for £10 million petrochemical installation in the Arabian Gulf. Principal roles: Assisted in the prep-

aration of the original tender and visited client to present and win contract in the face of competition from 7 other companies selected to tender ● Designed training package for local operating engineers ● Designed the inventory and procurement reporting systems software for the plant.

1977–80
Delphic Software Systems Ltd.: Managing Director/ owner. I set up the company to develop software programs for computer games – a personal interest of mine. After two years of rapid growth, when it reached annual sales of £250,000 and profits before tax of £33,000, the company was forced into liquidation by the collapse of two of its leading customers in the recession-affected toy industry.

1972–77
Engineering Component Industries Ltd.: Systems Development Engineer (1974–77). Principal Achievements: Led team which wrote ARMREST program, now widely used in industrial robots and producing annual licensing fees of £200,000 ● Educated staff and management in potential of industrial robots.

Executive Assistant to managing director (1972–74). Principal achievements: Wrote program for a new method of presenting statistical data from departmental managers that enabled two members of staff to be redeployed at an estimated saving of £50,000 p.a. ● Designed new systems for the analysis of company's marketing performance ● Accompanied managing director on several overseas business trips and wrote his background briefs for multi-million £ project presentations.

1967–70
Southern Radio Industries Ltd.: Product Engineer. Principal achievements: selected to go on tour of USA to review plants there and as a result instituted new procedures that cut wastage rates by £150,000 annually ● Devised and instituted maintenance programmes that reduced downtimes from defective working by 20 per cent ● Member of three-man team supervising a major factory extension.

INTERESTS
Sailing – have own 5.5 metre dinghy
Music – keen amateur cellist
Program writing – have devised and marketed a number
of my own computer game programs

This presentation is clearly a far more impressive document than Lawrence's previous effort and though he is,
perhaps, luckier than most in his high technology background anyone – literally anyone – has some sort of trump
card in his or her hand. It can be found by simply taking
what is there already in your self-assessment and self-
analysis exercise and selecting those aspects that are going
to interest the person sifting the applications.

It does not shirk any issues. Thomas Lawrence started a
business which went to the wall rather quickly. Most
people have some sort of accident black spot in their
careers. There is no need to go into tortuous explanations –
indeed in talking or writing about one's setbacks it is
important to bear in mind what Disraeli said was a golden
rule for politicans: never explain, never apologise. What
has to be done in such circumstances is to fit the event into
the career pattern so that it makes sense: in this case a
job-related hobby leading to a shot at self-employment.

Anyone can do this sort of thing for themselves, provided
they can angle their CV imaginatively towards what the
reader will be looking for, consciously or unconsciously.
Broadly it is for someone who can:

- Cut costs
- Get things done more quickly
- Increase sales
- Make the boss look good
- Improve performance
- Provide more information
- Beat competition
- Speed up delivery
- Cut down time
- Increase profits
- Work to deadlines
- Find new markets

Those aspects should emerge, not only from what you
have done in your various jobs in isolation, but also in their
relationship to each other. Hugh Roc tells of a friend who

consulted him after she had failed to make it even to the interview stage in a number of publishing jobs where she felt she should have had a reasonable chance. 'She'd done all sorts of interesting things in her life which were relevant to the editorial job she was after,' said Roc. 'But her CV presented them as more or less unconnected incidents. Employers want to see a story, a thread of progress running from one job to the next. The person who's doing a sift among 100 CVs to find eight or ten applicants worth interviewing won't stop to puzzle out a pattern. It's got to come over on the page.'

The role of the CV in interviews

Apart from its value in getting an interview at all, the CV is often used as the agenda for the interview itself. We will deal with interviews as a separate subject in Chapter 11, but suffice it to say that the one piece of documentary evidence that the interviewer has in front of them is your CV. In this sense it is like an examination paper to which you have seen the answers, but the examiner only knows the questions.

Most of the questions arising in the course of an interview will be based on facts in your CV. If you prepare yourself accordingly you will go into the interview with an almost incalculable advantage.

Some professional CV writers, as well as some consumers of CVs – recruiters and personnel people – think you should omit hobbies and interests from it. Equally there are those who advocate putting them in because otherwise you might emerge as the sort of boring automaton who finds it difficult to relax. The consensus, however, is that you should only list interests about which you are able to talk intelligently – you could be sunk within sight of the shore if you, put 'sailing' down as a hobby and your knowledge of it is confined to having done a bit of crewing on the odd summer afternoon, whereas the interviewer turns out to be a keen yachtsman. Preferably also there should be some coherence even in your hobbies – don't put down more than three or four and avoid weird mixtures like that seen on a recent CV – Golf, Powerboat Racing, Theatre, Music!

The 'No-career' CV

What do you do if you have no career as yet? If you are a

recent graduate in his or her first job or indeed if, like so many people in their early twenties, you have not yet worked at all? In this country it is more common to produce letters of application in such circumstances, but it is perfectly possible to concoct a CV from your self-assessment process. Where your academic attainments are non-vocational (e.g. in the humanities and some social sciences), the interviewer is looking, among other things, for additional qualifications that might be useable in a job – fluency in another language, for instance; even the ability to drive a car is worth a mention.

However, there is no need to feel apologetic about having taken a course that is not of obvious practical value. In fact, economic circumstances and technology itself are in such a state of flux that what may have appeared to be a relevant course at the beginning of your further education could be less marketable by the time you come to the end of it. Personnel managers (or manpower planners, or human resources managers, as they are coming to be called) are very conscious of this instability in purely functional demand and look for qualities like flexibility and adaptability at least as much as for relevant degrees and academic attainments.

How can you demonstrate such personal qualities, though? Principally by having done interesting things: in the contents of your course – particular and original lines of investigation and research, for instance; in your university or college activities outside the lecture room; and in holiday jobs, paid or unpaid. Even unusual holidays (back-packing across the USA? spending the summer in a Kibbutz?) are worth a mention. So are student activities which have enabled you to demonstrate leadership and organising ability, though political ones need to be handled with some discretion. Assume, unless you know it to be otherwise, that any employer will be conservative with either a big or a small C.

Even the way your CV is composed can be a positive factor – a capacity for clear, concise and jargon-free expression and the ability to analyse a sequence of events in such a way as to emphasise the important and persuasive ones is a significant part of any executive role. Signs of any gifts in this direction will make an impact on whoever reads your CV.

As for presentation, handwritten CVs are more likely to

be acceptable from recent graduates than in later job applications; which is not to say that typed ones are not preferable. Indeed, typing is a useful additional skill, especially now that the new technology involves keyboarding at every level. What is vital, but frequently overlooked, is neatness and if you have not encountered that pre- requisite since your schooldays prepare to have a chance that your interviewer would probably give his eye teeth for: re-live them in producing your CV. Nothing is more off-putting than scruffy, ill spelled ones. They will give the recruiter hours of opportunities to sound off about the failures of higher education, but they are unlikely to be so grateful to you for giving them an easy conversational gambit as to offer to see you, unless you can combine your offhand approach with some luring qualification, like a first class honours in computer science.

CV FORMAT FOR GRADUATE JOB HUNTERS RECOMMENDED BY PER
(reprinted by permission of *Graduate Post*)

Job applied for _____

Consultant _____ PER office _____

PERSONAL DETAILS

Name:	Jane Katherine Smith
Date of birth:	20 January 1960
Marital status:	Single
Health:	Good
Address:	26 Oscar Road, Cardiff.
Telephone number:	0732 4994 (term time)

If you are still a student, it would be helpful to give your term time address as well as your out of term address, with dates indicating when you can be contacted at each.

CARREER HISTORY

Education and qualifications

Give brief details of your education from the age of 11. List subjects passed at O and A levels, indicating your A level grades, as well as detailing your degree course subject(s).

Sept 71 – July 78	Oakwood Comprehensive, Cardiff. 9 O levels: physics, mathematics, chemistry, biology, English language, French, history, geography, art. 3 A levels: physics, (B), pure mathematics (B), applied mathematics (C).
Oct 79 – June 82	University of Aston in Birmingham. Degree subject: electrical engineering. Awarded second class honours BSc (Eng).

Work experience/industrial training

June 82 – to date	The Oak and Ram, Cardiff. Employed part-time to undertake normal bar duties.
July – Oct 81	Aston University/Aerodynamic Systems Ltd (combined project) work involved construction and testing of remote control measurement probe for analysing turbulence in turbine blades. (Planning for this began as a University project in the Spring term.)
July – Sept 80	Export Electronics Ltd. Quality control department. Work involved performing environmental tests on RAM and ROM and computer processor modules.
Sept 78 – June 79	Cardiff Area Health Authority. Filing clerk in Medical Records Office.

Include all work experience, even if it seems irrelevant to the jobs being applied for. Vacation work can indicate a good deal about your resourcefulness, your non-academic skills and your ability to function effectively in a working environment.

INTERESTS

At University I was captain of the Women's Swimming Team and a member of the Amateur Dramatic Society. Other interests: motor cycle maintenance, painting, science fiction.

This section should tell employers something about your personality, as well as listing any positions of responsibility you have held.

OTHER INFORMATION

I hold a full car and motorbike driving licence. I can type and I speak good conversational French.

Consider whether you have any skills or qualifications which have not been included elsewhere on your curriculum vitae. You might also wish to use this section to state briefly why you feel you are particularly suited to a vacancy.

83

8. Reading the Hidden Language of Job Advertisements

If all advertisements followed the principles laid down in the Institute of Personnel Management's recent publication *Recruitment Advertising*, the job market would be a simpler, though perhaps less interesting place. A good advertisement, the author says, should clearly set out what the job consists of in these terms:

1. The job title or the nature of the job
2. The location
3. The organisation – its size and what it does or intends to do
4. The job – why it is advertised
   - to whom the person appointed will be responsible and what his or her duties will be
   - what its interesting features are
5. The requirements – age
   - education/experience/qualifications
   - management or job-specific techniques that will be called for
6. Incentives – pay
   - benefits
   - working conditions
   - prospects
   - travel
7. Action required – phone
   - letter of application
   - send CV
   - send for application form

Rather rarely does one actually find advertisements that largely meet these criteria – here is one from *Executive Post* that is a model of clarity:

GENERAL MANAGER (Private Builder)
c. £10,000 + car   South Manchester

Our client is a small private company undertaking a wide range of building contracts including factory maintenance, home extensions, L.A. grant-work, and some private development.
The company now needs someone with good all-round building and man-management experience to take over the day-to-day management including labour utilisation, industrial relations, customer liaison, materials ordering, job evaluations, and managerial administration.
Aged between 25 and 50 you must have some knowledge of quantity surveying, job programming and be able to carry out simple levelling and setting out. It is preferable that you are qualified to HNC level in building or above or hold professional building qualification, but most importantly you must be able to demonstrate first class management skills and possess the personal qualities essential for running an efficient and profitable business. In return for your commitment, enthusiasm and effort to the success of the company an initial basic salary of c. £6,500 + profit share bringing expected earnings in the first year to c. £10,000 + company car and good prospects are offered.

If you know you can make a success of this excellent opportunity please write with full career history to Jane Entwistle at XX's Manchester office.

It says what the company does, where it is, what the job entails in the way of tasks, what kind of experience and qualifications these will call for and what the rewards will be. It also establishes clearly what the mandatory requirements are: 'must have some knowledge of quantity surveying etc ... must be able to demonstrate first-class management skills'. The secondary requirements are professional qualifications and if you can produce those in your CV all the better. The main thing, though, would be to structure your CV in such a way as to show how your 'first-class management skills' have embraced the range of tasks which 'the Company now needs'. The use of the word 'now' suggests that they are expanding into operations on a larger scale, so they would want to have facts and figures of three or four big building projects which you have supervised or played a leading role in, the range of sub-contractors you worked with, the number of men employed, the completion periods, the cost and time targets achieved or exceeded, and so forth. They would not want to know everything you have ever done, though – just a selection to whet their appetite. As Piers Wemyss put it:

> A letter or a CV in reply to an ad is to get an interview, not the job itself. The point is to arouse curiosity – the reaction 'here's someone I ought to see'. Don't go into enormous detail – always hint at the fact that you've got even more to offer. Say the essential things – the way you fill the 'must' requirements – but don't waste all your ammunition.

The clear way in which that job in *Executive Post* has been advertised suggests that it was drafted by the person in the company to whom the eventual appointee will be reporting, or at least by a good copywriter who had been thoroughly briefed by that person. This is by no means always the case. Below the more senior levels, advertisements are often written by personnel departments within companies and it is clear from their high 'noise to signal ratio' (i.e. more waffle than facts) that they are rather hazy about what the job actually involves. A good example, necessarily somewhat disguised, is the following advertisment placed by a brewery company:

CREATIVE
SELF-MOTIVATED
ARCHITECT

Rick Laren Ltd are looking for a Senior Architect to lead a small but highly professional architectural team at our H.Q. The team works with the Retail and Business development teams on development of properties in a wide area of South-East England. The scale and scope of the operation provides plenty of opportunity to fully exercise creative and professional skills.

The work undertaken ranges from the production of feasibility sketch schemes to the implementation and completion of contracts. The aim is the continual assessment and improvement of the image, suitability and effectiveness of properties to enable them to achieve their maximum potential through creative, cost effective, design.

Candidates must be good communicators, who are personally motivated by the opportunity to express their own concepts of design in a highly competitive area. The preferred age range is 28–35. RIBA qualification is mandatory and the ideal background would include a period leading a team within the leisure or associated industry dealing with contracts up to a value of £1 million.

Salary in the region of £11,000 will be offered and a range of company benefits include BUPA, a car and generous holiday entitlement.

Please write with concise details of experience and qualifications to:
Management Development Co-ordinator.

Few architects would describe themselves as anything other than 'creative' and 'self-motivated' but, reading on, they would be somewhat at a loss about the job itself. For one thing the salary for a 'senior architect' with experience of specialised contracts up to £1,000,000 is at any rate modest, which may cast doubt on the status of the appointment and hence the freedom to express, in reality, the 'creative and professional skills' the ad calls for. But what sort of work would he or she be actually doing, to which the CV or letter of application could be keyed? Is it mainly designing new buildings or re-furbishing old ones? Or a mixture of both? What is meant by 'leisure or associated industry'? It covers a range so wide as to be almost meaningless.

In fact, the only mandatory qualification is the basic RIBA one – membership, by examination of the Royal Institute of British Architects – and advertisements of this kind, though off-putting inasmuch as they indicate a lack of clarity by the advertiser, do give more scope for reply than a tightly worded specification. All they really know they want is an architect 'in the region of £11,000' (which means they will pay more). To be cynical, they are asking to be blinded with science and since the job is for a 'team leader', the chances are that there will be no one around to press you closely on any claims you make about the work you have done.

It would not be difficult to find other instances of jobs where the advertiser is really only looking for a technical or professional qualification and where the rest of the job specification is pure padding. It is generally a sign that the person who has written it is not really sure what the job entails or, in many cases, what the remuneration ought to be. Some sharp-eyed readers of job advertisements have already collected examples of the tell-tale words and phrases that indicate this kind of situation. They include such – apparently true – gems as an advertisement headed EXPANDING CONTRACTING COMPANY and a specification which called for 'a self-starter with motor industry experience' but apart from such delightful absurdities, there is a broad range of favourite meaningless words and terms:

Good commencing salary (actually the bad habit of not stating the salary is spreading here from the USA, where a figure is rarely given in executive job ads)
Attractive fringe benefits
Competitive according to age, qualifications and experience
Stimulating/Rewarding/Absorbing work
A Challenging/Interesting position
Exacting standards
A forward-looking company

Sometimes the use of such words – and any practised reader of advertisements could add to the list – does convey a hidden meaning. 'Fast moving' for instance means that the company is in some area of mass market products where success is dependent on high pressure salesmanship. 'Rapidly growing' indicates that they are not yet well-established in the market, though a firm which describes itself as both 'well established' and 'rapidly growing' is probably one that has recently undergone a change of management, especially when the 'environment' (another favourite advertiser's cliché) is also described as 'progressive'. If as a result things are lively but fairly chaotic, they probably call for a 'self-starter' which means nobody is going to give you exact instructions what to do, but you will be judged by results. It might also mean that nobody will quite know what to do with you when you get there, since the last incumbent left in a hurry and they have not quite figured out what he or she was doing.

Generally, though, there is a basic requirement somewhere to which a letter or CV can respond intelligently – but not always. Some advertisements are so vague as to leave the reader almost completely in the dark about what the job actually is. The laws of libel prevent one from illustrating such examples, but one that recently appeared was headed, COULD YOU SELL THIS CONCEPT? It called for people between 27 – 40 who needed to be 'well educated, articulate and able to mix well at all social levels'. No salary was stated nor what exactly the 'concept' was. Another of the same ilk was headed ENTRE-PRENEUR. It was on behalf of a company that described itself as 'being in the business of making money' and it called for people under 26 who 'have already gained distinction in whatever field they had chosen' and who would be able to 'effortlessly impress at all levels of commerce and society'. Again, no salary was given but since the advertisement warned that successful careers do not usually start off with big initial rewards, the implication was that it would be modest – which seems a bit hard for anyone who had gained distinction by the relatively tender age of 26 and who was expected to move effortlessly at all levels – a mode of location that is usually oiled by a large expense account, at least.

Yet another was headed, CAREER OPPORTUNITY IN MANAGEMENT CONSULTING. No salary, but 'essential for success' were stated to be the unsurprising qualities of 'ambition, hard work, dedication and integrity', though no other qualifications were called for. This advertisement at least did leave one in little doubt that 'consulting' was in fact some sort of selling job and one suspects that the others were too. Frankly, though, such advertisements should be approached with great caution even – or especially – by those who are desperate for a job of some sort; particularly when replies are to a box number, as they often are in such cases. They may not involve anything more harmful than selling – often on commission only – something that is not easy to sell to people who do not much want it. More dangerously such advertisements also signal sharks looking for anxious people with money to invest – particularly when they imply that age is no obstacle. There is a sucker born every minute, and not all of them are infants. The quality of the newspaper in which it appears, incidentally, is no guarantee that the advertisement will be above board. Though reputable papers do not accept advertisements if they have reason to suspect that readers will be misled by them, it is obviously impossible to check this until there is evidence of the fact – by which time it is usually too late anyway.

Another reason why the advertisement is less than clear would be that the advertiser is not really interested in filling the job at all. He may be using it to bamboozle competitors by hinting at a move into a new product area – perhaps in order to throw him off the scent of what he is really up to, in the knowledge that companies study each other's job advertising quite closely for intelligence-gathering purposes, to the point – reputedly – of getting candidates in for interview purely in order to pick their brains. Such bogus advertisements are hard for outsiders to spot, though recruiters claim to be able to tell them, as they also claim to be able to identify those where the aim is a 'fishing expedition'; simply to see what level of people apply for particular jobs in order to monitor salary structures for internal purposes.

There are also, so it is said by recruitment consultants, advertisements the object of which is to act as PR for the company who placed them, the signs being that they talk more of the virtues of the advertiser's product than of the job itself. This is somewhat hard to believe and may be due to the professional recruiter's low opinion of much of what they regard as amateurishly conducted in-company recruitment. Here is a possible example, though:

Sub Editor

Technical Times has a vacancy for an experience Sub Editor. Our weekly newspaper is less than four years old, and yet a recent readership survey showed that we are the most popular publication for the industry. We have achieved this through the quality of our editorial, not only in terms of content but also in our ability to present complex subjects in an easy to read, jargon-free form.

If you're a sub with a year or two's experience on tabloids and you can cope with this sort of challenge in a fast moving subs desk, you could be the person we're looking for. The ability to work accurately under pressure is important, and while we don't need technical wizards, the confidence to be able to deal with a technological industry would be a distinct advantage.

We can offer a good salary and conditions, and the opportunity to work on a growing newspaper which is constantly setting new journalistic standards.

What is more likely, however, is that jobs described in such glowing terms are often not all that attractive – the advertiser is trying to sell the job and indeed anybody who has ever worked in technical journalism will probably tell you that being a sub on that kind of paper is the nearest thing to the treadmill that the media provides. A good wine needs no bush and more or less adjacent to that advertisement was another for what is plainly a more attractive proposition, simply described in the following terms:

BERLIN
REPRESENTATIVE

We are looking for a Berlin Representative for the German Language Service initially to undertake training in London prior to taking up a two-year tour in Berlin. In certain circumstances the two-year tour may be extended. Duties include provision of material for use in German Language Service programmes, direction and administration of the local office, liaison duties and provision of news despatches in German and English.

Applicants must have good political judgement: journalistic and administrative ability and be able to broadcast in German. Familiarity with conditions in Germany an advantage.

Salary in Berlin within scale £11,990 to £14,915 p.a. free of UK income tax during tour in Berlin. Rent free fully furnished accommodation provided. An overseas supplement may be payable.

Contact us immediately for application form (quote ref. 2821/GU and enclose s.a.e.) **XY Appointments, London, W1.**

Usually, in fact, the reason why an advertisement leaves the reader in doubt as to what the advertiser is looking for is simple ineptitude. A common sign of this is where the company's activities are not described. That may be unnecessary where they are a household name – nobody would need to be told what Marks & Spencers do – or where the nature of the job emerges from the specification but where neither is the case it leaves you with a problem. What, for instance do Middleway Ltd. who, though not well known, describe themselves as 'an expanding and diverse group of companies with a current turnover of over £80,000,000' mean by saying they want a 'business development and acquisitions manager aged between 25 and 40 to handle the company's existing business and acquisitions'? Do not despair. Ring them up and ask for their brochures and PR handouts, though it is obviously inadvisable to admit that you haven't a clue who they are: tell them you want to get an up-to-date picture of their current activities, or some such thing. The information you get in this way will put you ahead of all the hopefuls who write in blind, who are likely to be about 75 per cent of the initial trawl of applicants. One of the reasons, incidentally, why such job ads are worth taking seriously is that they are often placed by smaller, family owned companies who are much more likely to be elastic about matters of age and even salary than larger, well-organised and hierarchical ones.

A very high proportion of jobs, though, are advertised through recruitment selection consultants – certainly above £12,000 or so. Partly this is due to the fact that design and copywriting for a job ad is recognised to be a specialist skill and that a badly worded, unattractively laid out advertisement is poor public relations for the company concerned. But the use of a recruitment consultant also has other messages for the job seeker. Recruitment consultants' advertisements, for a start, preserve the anonymity of the client (where an employer *is* mentioned by name, that means that the consultant is acting only in the role of an advertising agent and copywriter – everything else, including the selection of a shortlist, will be done by the client himself). At upper salary levels, the use of a consultant may mean that they do not have anyone in personnel qualified technically or in terms of status to handle the recruitment process. It could also mean that someone is 'for the chop' and that at this stage confidentiality is important. (Incidentally, the fear, often voiced, of applying for one's own job could not be realised with a vacancy advertised through a recruitment consultant. He would either ask you, in the ad, to state companies to whom you would not wish to apply or he would withold names of applicants from the client until the shortlist stage – and vice versa – which would, of course, give you the chance to back out in the event that you were applying for a post in your own company.) There may also be a less sinister reason for confidentiality. As we said earlier, advertisements are a source of intelligence to competitors and the advertiser may be planning a move into an area of business that he would not want his competitors to know about.

Recruitment advertisements placed by consultants are on the whole blander, less revealing and more professional than those placed directly by employers, but they are not entirely neutral either. In general, they will contain the kind of clear details that were listed at the beginning of this chapter, but even there, as more and more consultants appear on the scene, there are differences in expertise. There are also differences in writing style. Some are informal and rather sophisticated, like the example below. With a slightly joky heading, indicating that the job was for a middle range personnel person, it went on to describe the position like this:

> All right, so its a cliché – but sometimes the well-tried cliché is the best way to describe a situation. Corporate restructuring of a vast American conglomerate, a major piece of the world's operation centred in the U.K., a fresh awareness of the importance of personnel management, a newly-appointed Personnel Director (inheriting a very thin team) ... the end result has to be heaven-sent stimulation for a couple of experienced professionals, as they play their part in building a personnel function and in contributing to a personnel philosophy. At this point, not a great deal need be said about the company; it is one of those 'household names in consumer goods' you hear about, world-wide and profitable with its parent even more so! The gamble in joining this operation is a gamble on your own ability, not the company's viability. From the U.K. – conveniently to the West of London, with a possible relocation to improve facilities rather than fundamentally shift the home base – responsibility covers Europe, the Middle East and Africa. The two positions need proven experience both of the particular specialism and of international operations. The right candidates, probably mid/late thirties, will know exactly what we are talking about and appreciate the experience we need. Neither job is right for a generalist (whatever ultimate ambitions you may have) or for an enthusiastic amateur. However, there could well be an opening for a younger generalist, at the centre and a lower salary level, so we're not discouraging other applications. The senior positions are our major preoccupation – and we're hoping to hear from specialists with that unusual combination of genuine technical knowledge & experience, imagination and the work-rate usually associated (not always accurately) with U.S. operations. Please write with full career details to YY, quoting reference ZZ on the envelope.

Another, which appeared in the same issue of that particular paper, was from a firm who called themselves 'corporate consultants' and sported what appeared to be a coat of arms, though not, one suspects, of a kind that had been approved by the College of Heralds. It was for quite a good marketing job, but the description was riddled with clichés and pompous phrases like the fact that it had 'some degree of involvement in an international context' (probably export sales!). Plainly the two advertisements called for quite a different style of response, irrespective of the fact that the jobs were different – those same consultants would probably have phrased their advertisements in their own individual way, even if each had been handling the other's assignments. A witty, rather literate reply would probably get an interview in the case of the first consultant and one full of appropriate jargon would no doubt go down well with the other one, but either would go straight into the waste paper basket if they were reversed. Nor, one suspects, do those advertisements only reflect the attitudes and preferences of the recruiter. They would have been seen by the client, or at any rate the recruiter's general approach to things would have been approved by him. The style is the client, as well as his agent.

Beneath the style, though, there is the substance and here too there are lessons and messages which go well beyond the job title. The most important thing, from the point of view of the person answering the advertisement, is to distinguish the mandatory aspects of the job – the key requirements which you *must* have in order even to apply for it – from the secondary ones that are described in terms like 'desirable' or 'preferable' and which, though not crucial, do count in your favour if you can produce evidence of them in your letter of application or CV. Sometimes these are stated specifically in so many words, but quite often it is up to the applicant to sort them out for him or herself. Here, for instance, is an advertisement for a sales director's job with the subsidiary of a major British company:

The last ten years have produced an impressive record for our client – a record which proves the entrepreneurial spirit of both central and divisional management teams. Small wonder that our client is now a major British company with over 17,000 people in hotels, property, leisure and retailing.

XY is the most important of the leisure divisions. Yet another success, it is the market leader with 1,250 shops UK wide and a turnover of some £500 million.

The Sales Director will be responsible for all marketing and promotional activities geared to stimulating business within the shop network, but our client will also expect a broader contribution, outside of the marketing function, on the Board of the Division.

With a potential national sales force of 1,800 unit managers and 4,500 cashiers, the ability to work with and motivate operational management is of vital importance. The overall objective involves increasing still further the company's present market share, and the prime opportunities lie via:

1. The use of the company's market leadership to full advantage.
2. The identification of new products and presentation arising from research and the development of new technologies.
3. A new approach to advertising, promotions, merchandising and shop presentation.

These are the main components for the development of a new strategy for the company, which will require support to be won from all levels of the operation. In addition, the division is involved in expansion overseas which will provide new marketing opportunities.

It is paramount that the successful applicant is creative and resourceful. Candidates should preferably be a Sales or Marketing Director in a consumer goods company, where high brand image and aggressive marketing are key factors.

Age 30 to 40 years, with a degree or equivalent experience, applicants must be numerate, first-rate communicators, whose career record should show sound judgement throughout, balanced equally with creative flair. As would be expected, the position – which is based at Head Office in Middlesex – carries a superb remuneration package in all respects.

The function that is described as 'vital' is the ability to 'work with and motivate operational staff' on quite a large scale. Combined with this is evidence that the applicant is 'creative and resourceful' so that he can lead a sales team in a company that is both maintaining its market position developing new products. He is required to have ideas, to express them and to make them happen in the market; perhaps somewhere his career has included being a brand manager, an account executive in an advertising agency handling some well-known clients, and a sales manager or sales director somewhere else. The subsidiary qualities are that he (we have assumed that they are probably looking for a male applicant) should be a good administrator because of the size and range of the operation, that he should have some sort of experience of working with designers (because of the importance of the new approach to advertising, promotion and shop presentation that is mentioned) and that he should have another language and/or experience of working abroad because 'the division is involved in expanding overseas'.

All jobs are capable of being analysed in this way, though in some cases the secondary requirements are implied rather than stated. For instance, where a job involves being at the head of a large workforce, an ability to demonstrate skill in industrial relations would be an asset; for a training manager's post the ability to write manuals or, nowadays, to have some skill in making audio-visual presentations or producing videos would be a plus point.

However good your secondary qualifications, though, it is a mistake to apply for an advertised job unless you fulfil the primary requirements. There are ways of creating jobs for yourself in the unadvertised market, which we shall deal with in Chapter 10, but for an advertised post you will, in the words of Michael Armstrong, personnel director of Book Club Associates, 'have to meet the specification in three out of four points – and show how you can make up for the ones you don't meet.' You may feel that as a personnel man whose hobby is DIY that you know enough to run a sales force in the DIY field, but when such a job is advertised and you are in competition with people who have actually done it, your chances are slim. As one recruiter put it:

Employers aren't an adventurous lot. Anybody could drive a van who has a clean driving licence, but when it comes to hiring someone to do the job, they prefer it to be someone who has done it before to someone who might conceivably do it better but who is an unknown quantity.

Where the flexibility comes in is in your ability to fulfil the secondary requirements and if you can do that, some of the less critical parts of the specification begin to loosen. Age, for instance. If you can demonstrate that you can deliver most of the 'musts' and many of the 'shoulds' then you might find that 'between 25 and 35' stretches to 40 and even 45. You should certainly find that a salary 'in the region of £X' can be pushed up by 15 per cent and that where a range is quoted you can go for the upper end of it.

Whatever nuggets you glean from reading the hidden language of job advertisements would still be wasted, though, if you ignore the obvious. If they call for a short CV send a short one. If they ask you to write in for an application form, do not send a letter of application, much less a CV. If they ask you to send an SAE with your letter, do so; and, whatever it is, do it that week. In today's job market, queues form quickly and sometimes it can be a case of first come, first served, irrespective of merit.

9. The Job Brokers and What They Can Do For You

Finding the person for the job is a sizeable industry in its own right. As we said in the Introduction, the figures indicate that there are probably around 27,000 professional and executives jobs changing hands every month. Some of these are filled by internal promotion, but if you knock off 25 per cent for that reason and assume the average salary for each job to be £10,000 a year – which is probably on the low side – there is a market worth £200,000,000 a *month* of people who, for one reason or another, need people.[1]

Ultimately someone in a firm or an organisation will have to make the final decision about the person for the job, and an awe-inspiring decision it is. It has been estimated that the real cost of employing someone is twice their annual salary. The average time they stay in a job during the mobile period of their careers between 25 and 45 is about five years. So again, taking the low figure of £10,000 and assuming modest annual rises, one is talking about an investment of around £100,000. In more senior positions – say in the case of an MD with a 'Product life' of ten years – it is perfectly easy to get into an area where the figure at stake will be upwards of half a million pounds. No wonder employers want experts to hold their hands, to gather inside information, to check credentials, to sort out what they actually need, as compared with what they think they needed, to sound out second and third opinions, and (dare one say it) perhaps to share the blame if a misjudgment has been made.

The services of these experts are not cheap – if you include the cost of national advertising, filling a reasonably senior post will cost anything from £5,000 to several times that amount, depending on the method used – but even where companies have their own personnel department it is becoming increasingly common to turn to them. One reason for this would be if the job itself ranked high in seniority. To have someone interviewed by their eventual junior is obviously undesirable, even when the final selection is made by people higher up the echelon. There is also the risk of a recruiter not accustomed to selection at this level applying the specification too rigidly, so that someone who might be right for the job is eliminated on a quite minor detail. Confidentiality is also a frequent factor; either internally because the search may imply that someone is 'for the chop' or, externally, because impending job moves and new appointments are always eagerly studied by competitors. In the case, too, of the more technical job functions, the employer may feel that he simply does not have the specialised knowledge to judge candidates on anything other than personal impressions – financial appointments are often a problem in this respect. Finally, there may simply be a lack of time. Personnel departments have generally been slimmed down in the recession or been given a broader range of administrative responsibilities which make it difficult for them to handle at least the more complex and time-consuming selection and recruitment assignments. Even in a specialised area like accounting, a plum job can, as the recruitment consultants Douglas Llambias report, produce as many as 400 applicants. Though two-thirds can generally be eliminated without much further ado, they still have to be written to. The task thereafter of sifting the remainder down to a manageable short list is quite demanding in terms of administration alone.

For such reasons recruitment and selection consultants have proliferated in recent years, but they are only one of several forms of job brokerage which the person coming on the job market could encounter. Some of them are, as it were, on your side. We have already referred several times to career counsellors or consultants – two of the several descriptions applied to the growing number of agencies who act in various ways on behalf of people looking for executive jobs. There are also smaller firms who provide minor services to them – the professional CV writers, for instance.

Ranged on the other side are a whole lot of agencies who

act for the employer. There are the recruitment and
selection consultants whose services run from simply writing the copy for the job advertisement and selecting the
right media for it – acting as a specialist recruitment
advertising agency in other words – to the full service of
sifting the applications, conducting the interviews and
presenting a short list to the client. Above them, in terms
of rigour and accuracy of selection – at least they would
claim so – are the executive search consultants, otherwise
known as headhunters. They do not recruit on the open
market, but work behind the scenes, relying on contacts
and investigative methods first to identify and then to
approach successful executives, with the object of getting
them to move to their client. The selection and search
functions are not necessarily to be found in different and
distinct firms – in fact a great many recruitment consultants also offer executive search and it is generally thought
that the latter service is growing in importance and
popularity with clients. Although it is, on the face of
things, much more expensive than recruiting on the open
market, the cost of large display advertisements in the
national papers is narrowing the margins to the point
where the greater accuracy that is claimed for executive
search looks very attractive.

Between the consultants who act for you and those who
are retained by the employer, there is also a more neutral
form of brokerage – the appointments register. Here again,
some recruitment and selection consultants also maintain
a register, which is simply a list of executives on the job
market, with relevant details from their CV. These details
are circulated to prospective employers or, as is more likely
now that information retrieval is relatively easy to organise, extracted in response to specific enquiries. In some
cases these registers are not on a commercial basis at all,
but are a service to members of professional bodies who
find themselves on the job market. Finally, there are
agencies who specialise in finding temporary work above
the level of the familiar High Street employment bureaux.

Of these various kinds of brokers, all except career
consultants and CV writers act for recruiting employers
and are paid for by them.[2] The important lesson to be
drawn from this – and one which is often not recognised by
job seekers – is that it is very little use approaching
selection consultants or headhunters for help in finding a

job. Some of them are, in fact, prepared to give a certain amount of unofficial, free (though necessarily generalised) advice in such circumstances, but usually only if the person concerned comes to them with an introduction from a client, or is someone who has given them business in the past or is senior enough to be indentifiable as a source of business in the future. This advice will not, though, in any sense be a short cut to the shortlist. It is more likely to take the form of suggesting methods and avenues of approach, of possible job leads, even of industry gossip. Headhunters, for instance, have fairly pronounced views on some career counselling services who, of course, push clients their way if they know a search is on. They are inclined to take more notice of the suggestions of some firms in this field than others, though preferences may be a matter of style rather than substance. All such information is useful to the job seeker. However, before you can make sense of the job broking scene and identify ways in which it can help you, it is important to know more about what the various firms in it actually do and how they operate; a matter about which the average job seeker is reportedly very hazy.

Career Counselling

One reason why there is some confusion in this area is because of the proliferation of ways in which roughly similar services are described. For the purposes of this section we will use the heading above, but in a book which lists some of the main firms in the field, (Fred Kemp et al., *Focus on Redundancy* Kogan Page, 1980) there is a table, produced, one would guess in response to a questionnaire, in which these organisations variously describe their activities as follows:

- Career counselling
- Career and personal development
- Career management
- Redundancy counselling
- Assessment, research and development counselling
- Careers advising and job searching services
- Counselling and job hunting
- Career development counselling
- Career change counselling
- Outplacement

To some extent these terms reflect differences of emphasis or clientele. 'Outplacement', as already noted, is a service offered to *companies* to help them assist redundant executives to find their feet in the job market. One such firm (Sanders & Sidney) will only take on individuals that come to them through a corporate initiative of this kind, but the majority have a mix of purely private clients and those who come to them through corporate channels, though the proportion of that mix, again, varies from firm to firm. Some services are pitched quite clearly at those who have been made redundant while others again deal with career problems in a more general sense; those of people, perhaps, who feel they are on the wrong track and need careers advice based on more or less formal testing procedures. Even with firms that offer a complete service from initial counselling to helping their clients evaluate and negotiate the eventual job offer, it is sometimes possible to tailor the emphasis to individual needs – to buy only part of the service, in other words. Then again, there are firms that operate at the top end of the salary range, like Jack Barnes's Minister Executive and those that counsel people at middle and supervisory levels: John Kellet's Personal Counselling and Executive Careers, for instance.

Beyond that there are differences of emphasis in the way the counselling process is conducted. For instance, Frederick Chusid & Co., originally an American firm who were one of the pioneers of career counselling in the UK, are widely considered to attach a great deal of importance to psychological assessment procedures which, according to some of their competitors, have a somewhat over-analytical slant. Whether this criticism is justified or not it is impossible to say, but Chusid do not appear to be any less thorough in their methods, less well equipped or less comprehensive in what they offer than other reputable firms in the field.

A rather more bluff approach is personified by Tom Carew, the highly respected and popular head of Percy Coutts & Co. Ltd., who sees the problem as being primarily one of marketing, when he says:

Getting a job is all about marketing yourself. It's just as important a skill as any qualification and we don't, as a country, pay enough attention to it. Even MBA courses are hopeless when it comes to showing people how to market themselves.

Carew, in fact, is very much a believer in self-help, or at any rate in training his clients to help themselves – teaching the techniques of self-marketing, and eliminating, in a fairly down-to-earth way, the sort of things, ranging from mental attitudes to physical deportment that show up negatively in interviews. Another firm that advertises its services quite frequently, Interexec, take a somewhat different view. Whereas most career counsellors follow Carew's line in stressing, to a greater or lesser or degree, that the client has to do the work and that all they can do is to teach them the techniques and point them in the right direction, Interexec's claim is that in addition to offering counselling, they actually market their client through to the interview. An extensive network of intelligence about existing and upcoming job vacancies is maintained by a large staff of consultants making several hundred calls a week on behalf of their clients. Detailed, though anonymous, CVs are also broadcast widely and one certainly sees Interexec's literature around in the offices of headhunters and recruitment selection consultants, though it is fair to say that their claim that it is targeted carefully is disputed by some in the job industry. One suspects that their somewhat scattershot methods (they say they have some 2,000 'live' contacts in the market) would be most rewardingly applied to clients with no serious placement problem but perhaps a lack of time to conduct intensive job searches for themselves. Their brochure indicates – perhaps unintentionally – where they are at. It shows a clean-cut type of around 35, with an executive-style house in the background, a BMW in the drive, good-looking kids and well-groomed wife; not the way everyone sees themselves, but clearly the aspiration of a great many people.

There are also different views on how to handle the job search phychologically. Tom Carew, for instance, believes that you should roll up your sleeves and get on with it without further ado; a view which is not shared absolutely by another respected and successful operation, Forty Plus. They feel that one of the major deprivations of being out of work is its social dimension, so they provide an office for their 'members' – as they call the clients they are counselling. The office is a bit basic, rather like a staff room in a school, but it does have reference books, newspapers, desks, telephone and so forth. This means that the members have a base to work from, they can still 'come in to work' – which may be a psychologically important pattern to keep established – and they have the company of other members. The danger is that this can substitute chats and long pub lunches for action. On the other hand there are real benefits in having people around you with whom you can compare notes, who may previously have been interviewed by a person who you may be about to encounter in your job search and who, in any case, can collectively extend your network of job intelligence and contacts; quite apart from providing an element of companionship which at least bears some resemblance to normal working life.

Yet another difference between firms is the degree to which you are briefed and drilled before interviews. Some consultants provide packs which encourage you to rehearse every possible question that might come up, others feel that it is best to be as natural as possible. Such differences aside, though, there are criteria, which we shall come to shortly, by which the quality of a career counselling service can be judged. These are likely to become increasingly important as more firms get into the field, but at the moment it is probably fair to say that the choice would be more a question of horses for courses, or in this case, for jockeys. Personal impressions and 'gut reactions' count for an enormous lot on both sides on the fence in the job market. There are obviously people who would not fit into the image that Interexec projects, for instance, and vice versa. A rather sensitive person with a badly bruised ego would probably benefit from the sort of psychological build-up counselling offered by Chusid or CEPEC (Centre for Professional and Executive Career Development), whereas a tougher individual, perhaps someone with a sales background, would be happier with Percy Coutts. At more senior levels, the quiet approach and discreet methods of Jack Barnes's Minster Executive or Jim Smith's MSL might be what you feel most at home with. Industry specialists are harder to find, however. The only one appears to be Douglas Llambias Associates, a consultancy that offers a wide range of selection, headhunting and career counselling services in financial and accounting areas.

Such differences of style apart, there is not a vast amount to choose between methods, and this is also reflected by the fact that there is not a vast amount of difference, either, between what career counselling costs. Charges are around 12½–15 per cent of current or last salary and quite a number of consultants either offer a lower rate to private individuals or easier methods of payment. Search & Assessment Services Ltd., for instance, invoice employers who use their outplacement services at the start of the programme, whereas private individuals are allowed to make stage payments. Interexec will allow clients to 'stop the clock' under certain circumstances. For instance, if the client finds a job well before the completion of the programme, work done up to that point may be recalculated on the basis of an hourly rate. Yet another firm of consultants will base its charge to an individual on his or her 'salary trend', if their last jump was an extraordinary large one and there seems little hope that they can be relocated at that level.

Though it is possible, indeed advisable to shop around – and incidentally an initial consultation should cost you nothing – you are not likely to pick up any bargains, though it is worth checking the amount of the initial down-payment required and what you will get for your money overall: whether, for instance, some secretarial services are included in the package, or financial counselling. The object of talking to more than one counselling firm, however, is mainly to find out whether you can work with them and vice versa, because in a very literal sense you are putting your future in their hands. Even where your employer is paying for outplacement as part of the severance deal it is worth asking whether the final choice of a counselling firm can be yours. When you are working together with someone to help you find a new job or a new direction in your career, compatibility of their style with yours is almost essential. This is not only true of the counselling organisation as a whole, but also of the individuals within it who will be assigned to you.

Apart from their direct relationship with you, there is also the consideration that their corporate style is almost certain to be reflected in their range of contacts and in the way they suggest you should conduct the job search. If the one does not suit you because it is too brash, or too low key, too discreet or too forceful – or whatever does not go along with what you, in a current American phrase, 'feel comfortable with' – then it is highly likely that the other will be tarred with the same brush.

Not that career counsellors will pick up square pegs and force them into round holes. They nearly all stress that the process of actually finding a job is up to the client – all they will do is to direct his search, but they do claim to do so with almost universal success. One reason for this, as they will admit with varying degrees of candour, is that they do screen out lost causes. As Search & Management Services put it:

Prospective clients are screened carefully at the initial meeting and if we feel that our service is inappropriate we say so, giving what guidance and assistance we can.

People with a drink problem probably need a different sort of help from that which a career counsellor can give and there are also other cases which may be too tough to solve – the compulsive job hopper with no particular qualifications, the senior executive in his late fifties who will not settle for anything less than his previous astronomical salary are two examples that are frequently quoted.[3] On the other hand, career counsellors claim that a great many executives who come to them after months of fruitless and demoralising searches, feeling themselves to be almost unmarketable, turn out merely to have been making elementary mistakes in the way they have gone about things

The Career Consultancy Process

In some instances, an enormous lot can be achieved right away by changing clients' attitudes. Jim Smith of MSL reflects a general picture of what comes over at the first encounter with a counsellor in saying:

There's always some degree of demoralisation at some point if a person loses their job. It expresses itself in different ways – disbelief, rage, bitterness, hoping 'they' will change their minds. The phenomenon has been quite well written up now from research among people who've been involved in traumas of this and similar kinds. You can't send anybody out to be interviewed in that state, so I regard my first task as being to get people

107

to 'disidentify'. In that condition they are still identifying with their organisation – and 'how could they do it to me' syndrome. The first step is to detach them from the past and get them to start thinking about the future.

This process begins by encouraging you to think – but think constructively – about the past by listing your achievements. Ted Simpson of Sanders & Sidney who, in his role as a partner in a firm directly retained by industry to handle outplacement, often has the highly unenviable task of talking to executives who have been fired or made redundant immediately following the fateful interview, says:

I ask them to list a dozen achievements there and then. It's amazing what an effect this can have. It puts a man in a fighting mood by giving him back his sense of self-esteem. It also helps me, and him, by giving a prelimimary indication of the direction which his job search should take.

Not all this recording of achievements takes place in such dramatic circumstances, but it is a universal part of the counselling process. Percy Coutts & Co. ask you to write a 4,000 word essay about yourself. Chusid describe the same process as 'collecting an information base of background, experience, accomplishments and personality'. Minster give you an assignment described as lasting about sixteen hours in which you 'inventory your skills and experience'. Interexec, whose method of operation is probably the most different from that of its competitors, in that they go on to play a rather more active role in the job search by, for instance, sending out CVs to prospective employers on behalf of their clients, describe this as the 'consulting phase'; but its object is about the same.

At the same time a strictly practical exercise is also going on. This is a review of your personal and financial circumstances, needs and constraints. In some firms, expert financial and investment advice is provided, either as part of the package or as a separate arrangement. At this point too, they may ask to see your wife. Robert Baird, now the successful publisher of the *Journal of Executive Recruitment* (which, though aimed at headhunters, also contains a good deal of material of interest to job seekers in general) speaks from painful personal experience of undergoing a spell of redundancy in pointing out the practical and psychological family stresses it causes – a point of view echoed by counsellors and even the most cheerful and sanguine job seekers. For this reason, Ted Simpson says:

> We like to put the wife on the team. If she isn't part of it she can sometimes feel frightened or resentful. Looking for a job is a full-time occupation and you need all the practical and psychological support you can get.

Once the foundations have been laid, the next stage is to see what sort of building can be put on them. Here again career counsellors do the same things, but express them in different ways. Chusid talks of a 'unique ability analysis' in the course of which the client sits down with the counsellor to establish a pattern behind the achievements, somewhat in the way outlined in Chapter 5. Minster describes the same process as one where 'you and the counsellor examine together the work you have done with a view to filling in the gaps, elaborating upon the significant aspects of your experience, revealing hidden talents . . . your counsellor will highlight your strengths and assess their market value.' Ted Simpson puts it more informally:

> We ask our clients what they have done well and what they have enjoyed doing – the two are usually the same. It needn't be employment-related, though. To refine it further we ask them to rank what is on their list in order of importance.'

It is from this kind of information that you and the counsellor will be compiling your CV – which, as we have seen in Chapter 7 is essentially a quantified list of your marketable qualities – and, equally importantly, determining the direction of your job search. John Kellett, whose firm Executive Counselling and Personal Careers, has often been retained by PER in large scale executive redundancy situations, borrows a concept from Peter Drucker's *Managing for Results* in describing the possible directions of a search as 'additive', 'complementary' or 'breakthrough'. An *additive* search means simply building on existing skills and knowledge to look for a job similar to the one you held before. A *complementary* job move is brought about by looking at the unique ability analysis (or however you choose to describe the underlying pattern of your achievements) and trying to graft these on to a job in another area or in a related field which, while superficially different, is of a similar character. Drucker describes this in corporate terms as something which will, 'Change the structure of the business. It offers something new which, when combined with the present business, results in a new total larger than the sum of its parts.'

Applying this to the job search, John Kellett, gives an example:

> The marketing manager, having failed to get back into marketing, often decides his next option is to be a rep. This is clearly a step down in terms of status and, probably, salary, and an enormous waste of his experience. What he should be doing is to survey the range of tasks he has been involved in as marketing manager. These would include training, administration and personnel. He might have been involved in market research, in writing sales manuals, in organising exhibition displays or sales presentations. Everything he has done opens an avenue that either builds on an existing skill (additive) or is complementary to existing knowledge.

The ultimate option is the *breakthrough* which, in Drucker's words, 'changes the fundamental economic characteristics and capacity of the business'; in individual terms, this means using your knowledge and skills to do something completely different – work for yourself, go abroad, turn a hobby or an interest into a money-earning occupation.

Whichever of these roads you take, your course must in some way be based on existing knowledge if it is to be realistic. 'You can never make a Knight's Move,' says Jack Barnes, taking a metaphor from chess, where the Knight is the only piece that can vault over an obstacle to head off in a different direction. The complementary move can, however, resemble it closely. Jim Smith gives a classic example of a one-company redundant executive in his late fifties with a science background and a sound, but by no means spectacular career, the only marketable feature of which was that he had gained experience in just about every aspect of his firm's activities, from research to marketing. He was ultimately placed, at a higher salary than he had been earning before, with a finance company which was putting venture capital into a number of science-based projects but which absolutely lacked anyone with the background to evaluate them from a technical point of view.

Such moves are not always accompanied by salary increases, but one of their advantages is that they make the willingness to accept a salary *drop* credible. Jim Smith says:

> If you're prepared to drop in salary in a straight line move, employers tend to be suspicious, but it's considered quite acceptable in the case of a person making a lateral career move, or deciding on a physical move to another part of the country.

Determining whether your move is to be additive, complementary or breakthrough takes you into what Interexec call the marketing phase: how and where to look for the opportunities that the facts so far indicate would be right for you. You may be surprised to find that few career counsellors believe that there is much to be gained from answering job advertisements, at least as far as people over 40 are concerned. In fact, lack of success in the job search to date can often be ascribed to excessive reliance on this method. 'Only about 4 per cent of the people on our books get jobs through ads, so we don't encourage them to spend 80 per cent of their time in answering them,' says Ted Simpson. Not all his competitors take such a drastic view, but they do all stress the importance of the 'unadvertised job market', which is variously described as constituting between 50–80 per cent of the total job scene. We will deal with this fascinating topic in much more detail in Chapter 10, but what they mean is that rather than joining the queue that forms every time a job is advertised, you can by-pass it by creating your own opportunities. The method is to develop contacts, initially through the counsellor's own network, from which will grow a network of your own. It may be among executive search consultants (headhunters), recruitment and selection consultants or in actual companies – usually a mixture of all three. These contacts are not, it must be stressed, direct short-cuts to the shortlist, much less to actual jobs, though they may ultimately become so. In the first instance they produce only what are called 'contact interviews' or 'referral interviews'. Properly conducted, such interviews gradually build up your knowledge of the field in which you are searching, narrow down the nature of the opportunities in it to individual companies and people within those companies, while at the same time sharpening up your interviewing skills until a critical mass of knowledge and self confidence is built up which does finally lead to an offer.

In these later stages of the job search, the counsellor will probably have let you, as it were, take the wheel, though he is still on hand to steer you through problems. Before you get to this point, though, you will have got some fairly intensive coaching on basic techniques – how to compile a CV, for instance, how to phrase a letter of application, how and where to do background research before an interview. They also, of course, give you dummy interviews, and most of them now have video recorders which enable you to have the sometimes chastening experience of hearing and seeing yourself as others see and hear you. These techniques become particularly important as referral interviews gradually turn into job interviews and at this point your counsellor will move back into a more hand-holding role, ensuring that you are equipped to answer all possible questions and have eliminated any faults that may have sunk you on previous occasions.

Finally, they help you to evaluate any offer you have received and advise you on how to negotiate the remuneration package. Job seekers are apparently very bad at this and it is particularly a problem in the unadvertised job market because salaries are not, as in the advertised market, stipulated in writing. For this reason some counsellors say salaries should never be discussed in the interview, only the job itself, but others disagree with this view and say the issue has to be faced, though the candidate should never raise it himself or herself. Ted Simpson says:

> Where a job is unadvertised you can expect to be tested on this matter of salary. 'I don't think we could go that high' – that sort of thing, when you mention what you were getting before; particularly when times are hard and there's a lot of talent on the market. You shouldn't

taken an unacceptably low offer, but if it's thereabouts and you really want the job, try to insist on a salary review after six months.

This is a view with which most counsellors agree, on the grounds that if an employer has gone so far as to talk money he has probably decided that you are the right person for the job and is prepared to negotiate within reason.

Does all this sound too good to be true? I pressed numerous career consultants pretty hard on this point, particularly on the practicalities of lateral moves in the light of the fact that employers are, on the whole, not adventurous about taking on people who have not done something very similar before, but the universal answer was that, provided clients were prepared to put their backs into it, it works; very often resulting in an increasse in salary and very often within 5-6 months – about half the normal average at present.

Choosing a Career Counsellor

Career counselling in the UK has, however, grown rapidly from its beginnings in the sixties, when it was looked on with some suspicion, and though the firms in it at present seem to observe high standards, there is no guarantee that this will always be the case as new ones spring up. What criteria should you then look for, apart from this matter of style? The best and most reliable testimonials are likely to come from satisfied clients, so you should ask to be referred to some of these. Executive search firms also have fairly firm opinions about the merits of various career counsellors and are worth talking to and so are personnel directors of large companies who, in the nature of their work, are likely to come into a good deal of contact with career counsellors. Indeed, it is worth asking career counsellors at the initial meeting what *corporate* clients they have, as compared to those that come to them privately. The more of the former, the more highly they are likely to be regarded in the job market, and the more useful their contacts are likely to be to you.

It is also important these contacts are of the right kind. If you are an engineer, a counsellor whose background is in marketing will probably be of less use to you, however passionately he may claim otherwise. Most counselling firms have a brochure which lists their personnel and their backgrounds, though it might be worth checking how long they have been in the business – some firms are reputed to have quite a high turnover of staff. Even how they respond to your enquiry is an indication. One firm who was approached in connection with this book simply sent me a duplicated letter, unsigned, which bore no relation to the nature of my enquiry and which was accompanied by a fairly uninformative brochure. Personal impressions of this kind and individual judgments about the people you meet are as good a way of judging as any. Finally, and before you part with any money, there should be a written contract and its terms should cover everything that has been promised and agreed verbally about the nature and extent of the counselling service.

Career counselling, incidentally, is not confined to people out of a job or immediately likely to be so. At a time when most companies are reducing staff at all levels, the heights are more difficult to climb – and easier to fall off. Professor Hunt sees the hierarchy of companies changing their shape from that of a pyramid to that of a star. The chief executive occupies the tip of the star and the board and other senior executives fill the space between the arms below. But then the space again narrows abruptly, finishing in an obstruction, crowded with executives who may not be able to get further and whose jobs may ultimately be at risk. In that situation career counselling may be desirable and is actually sponsored by some employers. There are several cases – obviously confidential – of people in very senior positions now who went through counselling because they could no longer see a way forward in their previous job. Such executives, as well as other satisfied users of the counselling process, are likely to be the first link in the referral chain. Indeed, the degree of access to clients that have been successfully placed is another criterion for judging the quality of the service on offer.

Executive Search Consultants

Strictly speaking, executive search consultants, or headhunters, do not lie in the direct path of job seekers. They are retained by corporate clients to find someone to fill a specific position. Conducting a search for that person costs the client a fee of approximately one-third of the first year's salary for the appointment. Their relationship with the job seeker might therefore be described in the classic theatrical talent scout's phrase, 'don't ring us, we'll ring you'. Some of them are adamant in saying that they are not interested in talking to job seekers at all, but most admit to being willing to see them if they come with an introduction from someone they know and respect, especially if they are clients or potential clients or even potentially useful contacts. Contacts, and even gossip, are the name of the game in headhunting and if you can persuade them that you have some useful knowledge to impart, it may open some otherwise stiff doors. A case in point would be if you have a particular specialisation – the headhunters' own specialisations are listed in a useful book called *Executive Grapevine*, published by Baird Publishing Ltd, now unfortunately out of print, but you may find it in your library.

Executive search is becoming an increasingly popular method of recruitment and therefore an increasingly competitive one as far as the firms in it are concerned. Around 200 of them are listed, with a considerable amount of detail about their fees, conditions and personnel, in the publication we have just referred to. Many of them combine headhunting with conventional recruitment and the argument is advanced that, though on the face of things executive search is very expensive – one major headhunting firm, Eurosurvey, estimate the cost to be upwards of £10,000 per appointment – the real costs of conventional recruiting are also very high. A reasonably sized advertisement in the *Financial Times* and the *Daily Telegraph* will together add up to about £5,000, on top of which there are the recruitment consultant's fees or management time, if a firm is doing its own recruiting. Furthermore, it is by no means certain that the advertisement will actually produce the right person for the job, whereas headhunters will go on until they find him.

Though they do, frankly, prefer someone in a job to those currently out of one, the universe of talent is not so enormous that they can afford to neglect any part of it – especially now, when redundancy or the threat of it strikes as indiscriminately as the Black Death did in the thirteenth century. Certainly, many career consultants maintain close links with executive search consultants (closer than they would admit, probably) and vice versa, particularly when someone with a specialised skill comes on the market.

The Executive Search Process – And What You Can Learn From It

Headhunters, then, are a long shot in terms of actual jobs, but they are very much worth seeing and talking to, if you can get to them. One reason for this is that their method of operation – listening to gossip, analysing company news, ringing up individuals to sound out whether they would be open to an offer or know of someone who is – and of course their extensive network of contacts with client companies, their needs and problems, makes them an enormously rich source of information to the job seeker.

Another is that there is a lot to be learned from their methods that can be applied to the individual's job search. Indeed, when an executive search consultant is contacted by a client to find someone to fill a particular position, he is for the moment in the situation of a surrogate job-hunter himself. The sort of questions he must ask the client and the sort of job specification he must try to establish in order to direct his search correspond exactly to the range of issues that any individual working on his or her own must try to resolve about any company that they have in their sights.

In the first instance, the headhunter tries to piece together some general information about the client. What is the history of the company? What do they do, and how successful are they at it? How are they regarded by their peers? Is it a family concern, or at any rate strongly family influenced? Who are the executives who really make the running and what is their background? Have there been any recent significant appointments and are they likely to mean a change in any particular direction? What *are* the company's aims and objectives? Where do they see their growth areas and how do they plan to move into them?

From an overview of the company, the search focuses more closely on its internal organisation. The fact that it is spending a lot of money on recruiting from the outside rather than making an internal appointment may be significant in itself. Do they have a problem, and if so, what is it and how do they see it? (The two may not be the same.) Maybe the financial results provide some sort of clue. Or maybe the previous job holder did not turn out to be a success. Why? Is there some fault in the organisational structure, or some problem with the personalities involved that needs to be sorted out before the job can be done

effectively? Putting new wine into old bottles is a prover-
bially difficult exercise and many a firm these days recog-
nises the need to innovate, without being able to provide
the corporate environment or the resources within which an
innovator can operate effectively. Has the job, indeed, been
properly thought out? Consultants of every kind abound
with stories of how, having discussed a job with a company,
they were able to persuade them that the job specification
ought to be changed. A very alert and tactful job hunter
working on his or her own, having done the homework on
the prey, might similarly be able to persuade the company
that their real needs were something he could supply.

Defining and perhaps altering the nature of the particular appointment is in fact an important part of the
headhunter's role. He will spend a lot of time with clients
in establishing exactly where the job fits into the hierarchy, what the reporting responsibilities are, how success
will be measured and where it will lead in terms of
promotion and the general career development. There is
also the subtle and difficult question of corporate style. One
headhunter put it like this:

> It's not something that is easy to put your finger on.
> More like the sum of one's impressions. How do the
> senior executives dress? Do they go out of their way to
> take you to lunch in a good restaurant or is it shirt-
> sleeves and sandwiches in the boardroom? What sort of
> pictures and furniture do they have around? What time
> of morning do meetings start? Do they drift off at 5.30?
> That kind of thing is just as revealing as professed aims
> and objectives.

Another, perhaps typically British, part of this process
was described by one consultant who said, 'You don't put
someone with an Eton and Guards background into a
wholesale grocer in the Midlands.'

Related in fact to this question of corporate style and
climate is the style of the individual the client is looking
for. Do they want an aggressive entrepreneur or a quietly
efficient administrator? What sort of track record and
career progression is appropriate to the job? What age
should the right person be? Is it a position where the
appointee is being groomed for succession to someone or is
it, on the contrary, one where a person in a certain age

bracket might pose a threat to other executives and find themselves hemmed in, in consequence?

The question of salary and benefits comes, as always, at a later stage in the proceedings – not quite as an after-thought, but certainly as a reflection of the fact that if the company feel they have got the right person for the job, the matter of what is, after all, seldom more than one of financial semantics at this kind of level will not stand in the way.

To be headhunted is, as we have said earlier, the fortunate fate – usually – of those who still have a corpo-rate head on their shoulders, but there are ways in which you can make accidents happen. If you are earning more than about £17,000 a year, have a good track record, some sort of specialised knowledge and want to move, an intro-duction to a headhunter in your field – like well brought up Victorian ladies they will seldom speak to you without an introduction – is worth trying to arrange. It is unlikely to produce a job lead there and then, except in the million to one case where you walk through the door as a ready made specification, but it could pay well off at some future date as well as being informative now.

Recruitment and Management Selection Consultants

Though quite a number of consultants also, and perhaps increasingly, undertake executive search, orthodox methods are still the backbone of their business. A very high proportion of the jobs you see advertised, particularly at more senior and specialised levels, go through them.

There are several reasons for this, some of which are significant for the job seeker. One is that the administra-tive task of sifting dozens – sometimes hundreds – of re-plies is often best contracted out. So is the task of inter-viewing and selecting a shortlist. Line managers in a client company would probably feel that their time could be better occupied than with seeing candidates in order to eliminate all but a shortlist of four or six people – which is one of the main things recruitment and selection consul-tants do. They may also feel that the task of writing a job specification, designing and writing an advertisement and finding the right media for it is best left to the experts. Certainly, all these considerations would run through their minds if they did not have a personnel department of their own to turn to; and even if they did, they might still want to go outside it. The job might be too senior to be handled by a personnel manager – obviously no company in its senses would ask junior people to screen appointments senior to them; or it might be too technical – few generalist managers would feel themselves qualified to assess a senior accountancy appointment, for instance, and there are selection consultants who specialise in this or other fields; or there may be a degree of confidentiality involved, particularly if the job signals a move into a new field of trading or, internally, a switch at senior level.

All these are reasons why a company would route an appointment through a consultant even though, charging something like 20 per cent of the first year's salary, they are by no means cheap to use. But because one or other of these considerations often plays a part in the recruitment process and because personnel departments have tended to shrink in the recession, it is highly likely that the job seeker will quite often be dealing with an intermediary in the first instance.

What Recruitment and Selection Consultants Expect From You

There is nothing to fear from a good and experienced recruitment consultant – on the contrary, to be interviewed by a professional who can detect real quality under a nervous manner, for instance – has something to recommend it. On the other hand, they do expect you to present yourself in a professional way.

If they do not like your CV or your letter of application you will never get anywhere near the actual employer who has retained them and for this reason it is worth trying to find out what their preferences and predilections are in this matter of presentation. Unfortunately there is no uniform pattern in this – one consultant says that he hates standard letters and rather likes them not only to be individually tailored but also handwritten, others declared themselves to be reluctant even to look at handwritten material. This same consultant said that another of his pet aversions was advertisements stapled on to CVs, whereas others said that they found this practice helpful because it tells them instantly which job the client is applying for – a matter about which a consultant handling several assignments simultaneously is not always clear about himself at first glance. In the main, though, they are agreed that failure to supply essential details (it is by no means uncommon for people to forget to give their address) is an automatic thumbs down, as are signs that they have not read the advertisement properly; for instance sending in a CV, when all they were asked to do was to write in for an application form. Quite a number of consultants (as well as employers recruiting direct) use such forms because it enables them to organise the information provided by candidates in a reasonably uniform way. Another black mark is if these are returned covered in crossings out, spelling mistakes and so forth. A simple but useful tip if you get one of these forms is to take a photocopy and fill that out in rough before you tackle the original.

An amazing number of applicants get these things wildly wrong. Consultants are full of tales of long rambling letters and CVs (often in illegible handwriting) received from senior people applying for £30,000 plus a year jobs; riddled with explanations and apologies for this or that career move, instead of crisp, quantified accounts of achievements that are relevant to the job in question. But apart from avoiding such major mistakes, it is also worth finding out what sort of minor details of presentation turn consultants doing the preliminary sift on or off almost at first glance, because at some point you may want to apply for a job that they are handling. This applies particularly to the large firms who are involved in a high proportion of the jobs one sees advertised; also to specialist firms if you are yourself a specialist. Roger Stacey of Astron Appointments, for instance, specialises in publishing jobs and it is virtually certain that you will come across his tracks if you are in that line of business. The same is true of Douglas Llambias if you are an accountant. However, as is the case with headhunters, they are not keen to see job seekers unless you come with an introduction.

Appointments Registers

Quite a number of management selection consultancies, in addition to executive search, also maintain a register of people looking for jobs. They are shown in the publication *Executive Grapevine*. There is also one company, Lansdowne Appointments, that concentrates on this field. The idea is that the register is periodically circulated to client companies, or that it is 'searched' when a particular type of vacancy is notified and details forwarded to the client. This can be done with increasing speed and efficiency using computerised retrieval methods. As far as the client is concerned it is certainly the cheapest method of external recruitment. The question is whether it is any use to the job seeker.

The answer is that it depends. If you are at junior, supervisory or in some cases even middle management level (up to about £12,000 a year) and have some clearly identifiable specialisation, going on the register is worthwhile on the principle advocated by Charles Walker of the recruitment firm Charles Barker (who operate a register for DP personnel): 'try everything'. It will not cost you anything – the client pays. The crucial question is to whom and how often the register is circulated and what the retrieval methods are. How effective either is likely to be will be shown by how good the questionnaire from which your details are taken is – and indeed whether they have a questionnaire at all. Above all, of course, it is important to ask how often people on the register are actually placed in jobs.

Registers are quite popular with some professional bodies who maintain them to put any clients that may approach them in touch with members who are looking for work. A typical instance is the Society of Industrial Artists and Designers (SIAD) who get about ten enquiries a month from people who want to contact designers. They usually have about 200 names on their register – members who either want full-time jobs or who are looking for individual professional assignments. Sometimes they are approached by employers before they start advertising – which, as we have pointed out is always an expensive exercise – to see if they have anyone suitable on the register. It also happens that employers turn to them because advertising has not produced a suitable candidate.

The sort of people who get jobs through the register –and one suspects that in this respect SIAD is not untypical – are younger designers with 3-5 years' experience in the middle salary range. There is less demand for beginners and for older people in the upper salary group the tendency would be to advertise or even go to executive search; which is not to say on the 'try everything' principle, a professional association's register should be neglected. Jean Harding who runs the SIAD register realistically sums up its value in saying:

The people who come to see our association as one of several things do find work and are usually successful in the end. Sadly there are a lot of people around who think they can leave it all to someone else.

As in this case with commercial registers, though, the indicator of how useful a professional association's register is likely to be is how professional their questionnaires are and how effective their client contact is. The form the SIAD sends out to clients seems a model in this respect and anybody using a professional association's register as a means of finding work would be well advised to make comparisons.

To find the right designer fill in and return this section to: **SIAD Designers' Register, Nash House, 12 Carlton House Terrace, London SW1 (Telephone 01-930 1911)**

I am interested in finding a:	Freelance designer ☐ Retained consultant ☐ Staff designer ☐	I am looking for a designer with previous experience related specifically to:
with experience in:	Product Design ☐ Fashion Design ☐ Textile Design ☐ Interior Design ☐ Exhibition Design ☐ Graphic Design ☐ Engineering Design ☐	_____ _____ Name _____ (Please use block capitals) Position in company _____ Address _____
located in:	London ☐ South East ☐ South West ☐ Midlands ☐ North East ☐ North West ☐ Scotland ☐ Location not important ☐	_____ _____ _____ Daytime telephone number _____ Signature _____ Date _____

Professional and Executive Recruitment (PER)

From an employer's point of view, one of the problems of getting staff from a register is that unless it is kept absolutely up to date and 'dead' (for one reason or another) names removed from it, he may find that the person he is interested in is no longer available (or indeed may never have been available at all – he or she may merely have been 'window shopping'). That certainly came to be the case with the old Professional and Executive Register. The word – and the service – has now been dropped and PER's reputation is slowly recovering, while at the same time it has become more cost effective. This has been done by putting the initiative in the hands of the job seeker, where it does, after all, belong. You still fill in a form when you go to a PER office in search of a job – you do not, incidentally, have to be unemployed to qualify for PER's services – but what now happens thereafter is that you will receive their weekly freesheet *Executive Post*. This goes out to about 160,000 people, of whom 20 per cent are in a job and it contains 400–500 vacancies per issue, classified by job type and content. There is even a section for temporary jobs and for more self-employment opportunities – franchising, for instance. In general the jobs are junior, middle and supervisory levels at salaries of between £9,000 and £15,000 a year, though some overseas posts carry much higher rewards.

At this level, *Executive Post* is proving popular with employers and it now carries more job advertising than any other medium. Its standard rate – at the moment £225 per 250 words – compares very favourably with the astronomical costs of displays in other papers claiming national distribution. PER also offer a very competitively priced selection and recruitment service to employers, though how highly it is regarded depends somewhat on the quality of the personnel in the individual PER offices that are now scattered throughout the country.

PER also offer some courses, free to people who are out of a job or who are facing redundancy. There are half-day job-hunting seminars which deal with very basic techniques and explain what PER does and there are longer, residential Career Review and Development Courses. Details and venues of these and other PER-sponsored courses are given in *Executive Post* along with editorial features of interest to job seekers.

For more senior people PER is perhaps of limited value, though the editorial content of *Executive Post* is applicable across the whole spectrum. Furthermore, even though the upper salary level of vacancies *tend* to be around £15,000, there are occasionally jobs above that figure; reflecting, perhaps, the fact that fishing among the unemployed is no longer regarded by employers as a way of catching species that other anglers do not want.

The First Job Problem

Although job brokers agree that the older executive is not the problem he used to be – Forty Plus's re-employment record for the first half of 1982 includes three people (out of twenty-two) over 55 – the situation of those looking for their first job, certainly through orthodox channels is not encouraging. A much discussed series of articles in the *Sunday Times* in 1982 contained the information that one in six young people under 25 were currently registered as unemployed and a quarter of a million had been out of work for a year or more. The fact that unemployment among recent graduates could, according to an article in the June 1982 issue of *Graduate Post*, reach 20 per cent, indicates that at least in relative terms, their position is even worse.

This is a situation which would seem to cry out for job broking, but the difficulty is that brokers make their money out of a percentage, in this case salary, and if the salary figure is not large enough, the proposition is not attractive commercially. At school leaver level, the government's attempts to fill this gap have been disastrous. Few young people have a good word to say about YOPS (Youth Opportunity Programmes) or any of the other bewildering acronyms which offer a similar combination of subsidies to employers and a rather low wage to young employees for a limited period. They are widely regarded as a form of low paid labour which, except for a lucky few, merely leads to further unemployment at the end. As for jobcentres, they are universally criticised, for the same reason, in reverse, that the old Professional and Executive Register used to be: whereas in the latter case, the employee was often no longer available by the time the prospective employer had caught up with him, in the case of jobcentres, news about vacancies are not properly updated and applicants are very often sent off on what often turn out to be expensive as well as demoralising wild goose chases. As one young job seeker put it:

When you consider that every £2 someone on the dole spends is equivalent to £10 for someone taking home £100 a week, you begin to understand that even fares can be a real drain on the pocket.

Graduates, at least, are somewhat better served. They now have their own freesheet, *Graduate Post*, a junior version of *Executive Post*, which contains a similar mixture of editorial features, news about courses and classified job advertising. It has a circulation of about 75,000 through PER offices and Career Services at universities and polytechnics. The problem is that it does not go to recent graduates who, though employed in their first job, have not really found something that suits them. Reportedly, however, though, PER services are theoretically only available to those who are either redundant or threatened with job loss, they by no means turn a deaf ear to the needs of the increasing number of graduates who have had to settle for something less than their aspirations.

The fact is that for the first-time job seeker, this may be the only way into the market. The executive level of the Civil Service, once spurned by most people with degrees in preference for the grander and more highly paid administrative grade, is now attracting graduates, as are some professions, like accountancy, training for which people used to step into straight from school. Lower down the market, the sort of jobs that used to be regarded as suitable for those with O levels are now being competed for, often in large numbers, by A level pupils. The great disaster area, of course, is for those with few qualifications, or none at all. Qualifications *are* important at whatever level. One young man who used to subscribe to the myth that they do not greatly matter until he came into sharp contact with the realities of trying to find a job said:

Many graduates feel that a non-vocational degree is not much better than A's for job-hunting. This is not so. It is definitely easier for someone with a degree to get a job than for someone with A's, and so on, right down the educational line. As far as graduates are concerned, employers tend to 'buy a brain'. They think of all graduates as being reasonably bright and are not particularly concerned what subject a degree is in. It's the degree itself that counts, even if you can't actually use it in the job. In fact one of the problems that many career officers complain about is that people treat their qualifications as vocational when there are plainly very few openings in that field (zoology, for instance). This fault is most pronounced in people with A levels who are just entering the job market. Careers officers are constantly faced with those who want a job that puts their A levels to good use. The point is that A levels were never intended as qualifications for a job but as qualifications for entrance into university.

The advice generally given by graduates and school leavers who have been able to get jobs is to grab whatever is going, then move after a decent interval if it does not lead anywhere after at least a year, because employers are suspicious of anyone who stays for much less than that. The same young man who talked above about qualifications also said:

There is no doubt that being on the dole for long periods of time – over three or four months – seriously affects job chances, so do something, even if it is helping out at the local Oxfam shop on Saturdays.

The vital thing is to demonstrate job experience of some sort, both because it is in itself valuable to an employer to have someone around who at least knows what an invoice is and because it demonstrates an ability to get to grips with the difficulties of the present situation – difficulties that employers also share now, though they never had to in the days before the milk round became a slave market.

---

[1] Sceptics should consider this fact: one medium alone, the PER's freesheet *Executive Post*, advertises about 2,000 jobs a month – some £20 million's worth of executive income.

[2] Though the practice is growing for employers who make senior staff redundant to offer career counselling as part of the severance package. This is then known as 'outplacement' – but the employer is merely, in such cases, paying on behalf of the employee in question. From the latter's point of view this has certain advantages from a tax and VAT point of view.

[3] It should be said at this point that both counsellors and their clients are predominantly male. Very few firms appear to be employing female counsellors, which no doubt reflects the comparative rarity, still, of senior female executives.

10. Inside the Unadvertised Job Market

In Chapter I we referred to what might be called 'the curious case of the missing job vacancies' – the big discrepancy between the 40,000 or so advertised appointments in the nationals and the 300,000 or so professional and managerial posts which, so it can be inferred from the House of Lords Select Committee report on employment, change hands every year. Some of that large number can be discounted because of the rather loose definition which the Department of Employment attaches to the term 'professional and managerial'; furthermore, not all jobs are advertised nationally – a good many turn up in professional and technical journals only (usually the weekly ones) and some make a limited appearance in local newspapers. But even if one takes a jaundiced view of the DE's definition and says that 'real' professional and managerial jobs (as compared to what are probably supervisory posts which are being given the benefit of the doubt by the civil servants compiling the figures) are only half that number and that a further 50,000 vacancies are advertised locally or in the specialised press, that still leaves 60,000 professional and managerial posts to be accounted for. That proportion – 40:60 – is what many job brokers regard as the mix between advertised and unadvertised vacancies. Some, in fact, put the proportion of the latter even higher, claiming that at more senior levels as many as 80 per cent of jobs are filled without ever being advertised. But whatever the percentage is, no-one denies that the percentage of unadvertised jobs is very substantial.

But what and where are these jobs? Is there some black market in jobs that change hands under the counter? Or is there an 'old boy network' of such massive proportions that over half of the available vacancies are filled from the ranks of those who went to the right schools or universities; or is there again some secret treasure chamber of jobs, the key to which is held by career consultants in the same way as the key to certain exclusive London parks is held by their surrounding residents?

There is a grain of truth in each of these dark surmises. Yes, some jobs do change hands almost surreptitiously, not for money but because the right person happens to walk through a company's door at the right moment. Yes, there is such a thing as the old boy network and ties of association of *any* kind are thicker than water. Yes, career consultants do have some insight into this market and a large part of their stock in trade is to teach their clients what that insight consists of and how to develop it for themselves.

The good news is that there is nothing magical about this process. The unadvertised job market is all around us but we often fail to spot it because all our conditioning in the job search is to move along traditional and well-beaten tracks – usually a combination of flicking through the advertisements to see what job labels correspond to the label our previous job stuck on us, putting the word about among a few friends ('let me know if you hear of anything') and shooting off a few on spec letters to recruitment firms (they get hundreds every day, mainly from people who have no clear idea of what such consultants actually do in the market).

But, you might say, how else can you do it? De Bono's book, *Lateral Thinking*, again gives us a starting point. In talking about problems, he says that what generally stands in the way of our solving them is not only the absence of information but also the preconceived way in which we study the information that *is* available. The way out of this dilemma, he says, is:

> . . . to restructure the pattern by putting things together in a different way . . . the purpose of the rearrangement is to find a better and more effective pattern.

Tracking Down Job Leads

The pattern in this case is the job market and rather than looking at it as pages of advertisements, let us look at the situation which gives rise to these advertisements, thus, instead of asking the question 'what?' when looking at the appointments pages – a question which for hard-to-place job seekers will often yield the depressing conclusion that there is nothing there which they would stand much chance of getting – try asking 'why?'. Why are the jobs there at all? Here are some possible reasons, at least one of which will fit into every job you see advertised:

- *Expansion of an existing operation* – example: a computer company stepping up sales by going into mail order are looking for an expert in that mode of selling
- *Opening up a new market* – example: a company looking for an area manager in the Middle East
- *The development of a new product or service* – example: a software house producing programmes for computer-aided design
- *Move to a new geographical area* – example: an overseas company advertising posts in a newly established London office
- *The introduction of new technology* – example: an advertisement for a communications manager to be in charge of telecommunication facilities
- *New and recent inventions* – example: microcomputer and video companies starting up
- *Straightforward staff changes* – example: vacancy due to promotion, retirement or departure of an incumbent (deaths and dismissals are never given as reasons for a job becoming vacant, although both are common enough)

Getting Inside Information

Clearly, if you can anticipate such a situation before the advertisement that reflects it is published, you can bypass the queue of applicants that forms the moment it is. But how can you, as an outsider, get at inside information at this level?

Strangely enough, you can achieve a great deal by methods so obvious that most people overlook them. An interesting analogy to this process was described by a Polish intelligence officer who defected from his country's Washington embassy. Very little of what he had to do concerned coded messages, microdots printed under postage stamps or any of the accepted paraphernalia of intelligence gathering. His work consisted largely of diligently reading the newspapers and piecing together bits of information that meant very little in isolation but that were highly significant when put together. It was also amazing, he said, how much secret material was readily available if you knew where to look for it. His greatest coup – getting maps of the approach routes to every civil and military airport in the USA – was achieved by joining a military pilots' association (he gave his rank but no-one bothered to ask what army he was a colonel in!) and then simply sending off for all the charts they had.

In the same way an enormous amount of information relating to job opportunities is published every day for all to see who have the wit to see it. Here is a selection of job leads gleaned from a random survey of newspapers and periodicals at my local library on one afternoon in mid-1982.

On that day the lead story in the financial section of *The Guardian* had as its apt headline ONCE YOU LEARN TO BE INVENTIVE YOU CAN STAY AHEAD OF THE PACK and though this turned out to be an item about a building society, there were other items that were more promising from a job-hunting point of view. For instance, at the foot of the page there was a headline BIG HOUSE-BUILDING RALLY which showed that work on new houses for the first four months was up by 40 per cent on 1981: food for thought there surely for a wide variety of building professionals that now might be a good time to write to some of the larger contractors.

Over the page there was another story – this one about unemployment, the gist of which was the drift of jobs away from cities to rural areas and small towns 'on a scale which swamps most other trends in industrial locations . . . the winners are predominantly rural regions like East Anglia and the South West'. This suggests that a look at job ads in some of the provincial papers in these areas could have been fruitful.

The *Financial Times*, in their UK company news pages, had a wealth of job-related information through company reports and the FT's well-informed comments on them – the fortunes and plans of a variety of companies, e.g. a story on a share-tipping magazine that had done extraordinarily well – expanding its profits by 25 per cent. That would seem to suggest all sorts of possibilities to redundant executives from the stocks and shares fields, as well as to marketing people – maybe to approach a newspaper group with a suggestion for a competitor. On the next page, there was a story about a £300 million expansion programme by Marks & Spencer over the next four years. Surely competitors in the towns named in the article would be reacting?

In the company results section there was a story about a major cleaning company, with comment on the parts of their business that were doing well and also some news of plans to expand into the USA. Someone with experience of marketing in the USA who responded and referred to that kind of information would probably have got a hearing, and though he might not get that job, there might be something else going. In a progressive company he or she would at least get some marks for initiative.

The *Financial Times* has also an appointments column – potentially useful news of appointments and departures. Chief executives might find their friends here – worth an approach, possibly: it might produce a contact interview.

Campaign is an excellent source of information for anyone in marketing, advertising and communications. Here are some job leads to unadvertised possibilities in that week:

- CAMERA GIANT PUTS ONE MILLION INTO TV ASSAULT. This was a story about a Japanese camera moving into the SLR market – it's a fair bet that its rivals would follow suit in some way. Possible approach from someone with a marketing background?
- POLAROID IN NEW ROW AS CHIEF QUITS. This was a story about the UK sunglasses market which 'offers a great chance for established companies or newcomers to make a big impression'.
- An article, SEASIDE TOWN SWITCHES ATTACK, explained how Blackpool was allocating £100,000 to an ad campaign to run June–September to attract late bookings. Traditionally all such advertising had been done in later winter/early spring. An approach by someone with a marketing background to other seaside towns, e.g. Bognor, Scarborough, might have brought an interested response.
- FRENCH PATÉ SALES SOAR indicated a self-employment opportunity.

– Another article about a major housebuilder. It described how well he was doing – moving into sports sponsorship and some sponsored publishing. This report went on to say that they were doing very well with housebuilding in the North but had so far failed to make much impact in the South – but intended to do something about this. A whole range of jobs suggest themselves here to people in construction, in PR, to people who know about sponsorship. It may be all ballyhoo but the chairman would hardly disown this article and its implications if you wrote to him.

– A big report in that same paper on conferences and exhibitions was rich in job leads. Manchester and Newcastle were planning to open conference complexes – anyone who had had experience of organising such events for their company would surely have been given a hearing. One could also infer that exhibition – stand designers in those towns might need a product marketing person and manufacturers might need designers.

The *Architects' Journal* – which has a fortnightly column called 'Opportunities' that gives potential sources of work for architects – that week had a story about a venture by the Scottish Development Agency to move small firms into redundant buildings left by the jute industry in Dundee. One could ask for information about them.

The *Investors' Chronicle* also has a wealth of company reports and comment. Features in that week included an article about what investment analysts do, which suggests that somebody with the right economic, scientific or industrial background might consider this as a sideways career move. The job was described as follows:

The analyst studies the structure of the retail industry and patterns in retail spending. He looks at, say, Marks & Spencer. He studies its history, visits its stores, products, range, store location, market share. He looks at balance sheet ratios, cash flow, dividend potential. He then makes a forecast.'

The *Daily Telegraph* had much the same financial comment on company results but had a stimulating self-employment story about people who have set up a business doing antique valuations to help those 'sitting on valuable pieces they might otherwise consign to a bonfire or perhaps to a disreputable dealer.'

Apart from such specific stories, there are always general trends in the news which are worth thinking about in terms of their implication for jobs. Here are just a few found in the paper on that day:

- *New legislation* – The pitfalls of EEC rules and regulations into which companies fall daily could call for the services of someone whose possibly unenviable job it is to monitor the stuff that pours out of Brussels and Strasbourg.
- *New social problems* – In the 60s and 70s it was housing, now undoubtedly it is unemployment. But that also brings with it opportunities for those who can train people for all sorts of vocational skills.
- *New economic trends* – The decline and collapse of many traditional industries is causing companies who are still in them to look seriously at moves to other and healthier areas.
- *Changes in consumer habits* – What are the implications to cinemas in rapidly declining audience figures or for tobacco companies for the drop in cigarette consumption? It is a fair bet that companies affected by such factors would be interested to hear from anyone with a background in a growth industry.

Even job advertisements themselves often give away many clues about the needs of companies that placed them – needs that do not exist yet but where it may only be a matter of time before the implied becomes the explicit.

- A growing computer company may also need someone to write comprehensible user manuals – notoriously not a strong point with technical people.
- A firm that is expanding its exports may need a person with experience of dealing with shipping and air freight and evaluating options of price and delivery speed.
- A promotion manager, when he or she arrives, may decide that they want an in-house person to write copy and design displays.

133

– A new senior appointment at board level very often entails changes all the way down the line – especially if the company concerned is known to have problems.

None of these means that you should reply to advertisements for which you do not meet the specification with some letter to the effect that you can't do 'x' which they are asking for, but you can do 'y' which they are not. Job brokers of various kinds get such letters every day and they go straight into the wastepaper basket as do dozens and dozens of general on-spec approaches received with similar frequency by the chief executives of large companies – often not even addressed to them by name but beginning 'Dear Sir' – and saying something on the lines of 'I have just returned to this country after eight years in Quatar where I supervised the construction of a number of major projects. For personal reasons I would now like to remain in the UK and I am writing to ask whether you have any vacancies where my experience would be useful.'

To get at unadvertised jobs needs a much more systematic approach *the ultimate goal of which is to persuade some employer somewhere that they need you, nothing but you, and nobody else but you.* This process starts by asking the question 'why?' about job advertisements – uncovering market forces behind them. It goes on to fill in the details of those forces by careful research into the explicit or implied needs of industries and individual companies, partly by reading about them and partly by talking to people –piecing together like our Polish spy bits of information until a clear focus emerges right down to the crucial person in the individual company who could make you an offer of a job that will never be advertised. It will never be advertised because they will be convinced that you are the person uniquely qualified to fill that job and you will be in that position because through your research you will have identified that employer's needs and problems so precisely that you will have in a sense have created that job for yourself.

This is the technique which career consultants teach their clients but it is also one you can learn for yourself. Central to it is the concept of the 'contact' or 'referral' interview as it is variously known. So what is it and how do you set it up?

Setting Up A Contact Network

We have said earlier that there is a grain of truth in the notion of an 'old boy network'. The term has overtones of belonging to the society of those who went to the right schools and universities or who belong to the right clubs, and those who do not have connections of this kind are apt to comment bitterly that 'it is not what you know but who you know'. The fact is, however, that everyone knows or can think of contacts who might be of use in the job search. For instance:

- friends in good jobs
- customers
- suppliers
- fellow members of professional institutes or organisations
- business acquaintances
- recently retired executives
- former colleagues who have moved on
- former teachers or instructors
- professional advisers like your accountant or bank manager
- important or useful people whom you know any of the above to be acquainted with.

You can even add to that list people you do not know personally but whose achievements you admire or to whose organisations or industries you feel you could make a contribution. The list you end up with falls into a number of braod categories, each of which is to be approached in a difforent way:

- friends and close acquaintances
- people you know less well – business contacts and more casual acquaintances
- people to whom you can get an introduction through a third party
- people whom you cannot get at directly or indirectly but who you think you ought or would like to talk to.

The mistake that a great many job hunters make is that though they do have contacts and introductions they waste them by asking them straight out for a job or for a direct job lead. If no job is available – and usually it is not if you made the approach in that way – that closes the discussion.

Even if the person you are talking to is someone who had in the past asked you to let them know if you ever want to move, the chances are that when you do, nothing is available there and then.

At the other extreme there are those who for reasons of delicacy or embarassment drop vague hints that they are unhappy in their present job/that they might be made redundant/feel it is time they moved on for career or salary reasons and in general imply that they would not be averse to a good offer. They lose no friends that way but they don't get any jobs either.

The right way to use contacts is again to restructure the nature of your search. The question is not 'What jobs do your contacts have in their gift?' (to which the answer is usually 'none') but 'How can they steer you in the right direction?'. Once the problem is restated in that way, a whole lot of options open up; and because they are all matters over which your contact can *genuinely* help you, they will be infinitely readier to talk to you. Here are some things they can tell you that it will be immensely valuable for you to know about:

- news about firms where there are impending changes of staff, policy or location
- information about problems which company or industry is encountering
- opinions on opportunities of which a potential employer is failing to take advantage
- names of people outside the particular firm you are interested in who can give you more information about it
- names of executives in the firm whom you might eventually approach
- gossip on what a company you have in your sights is like to work for
- views on any particular aspect of your qualification or experience that an employer in your target industry or field might find attractive
- directions on what you ought to be reading to enhance your background knowledge or further training you could usefully undertake
- opinions on how realistic your aims are in terms of career or salary
- assessments of the way you are putting yourself over face to face and in writing

However, even this approach is not likely to be success-ful unless you make it clear what you are after and what you have to offer, otherwise you are apt to land up with the situation that is described – for some reason in terrible blank verse – in the American best-seller *What Color Is Your Parachute?*:

Time to go and see those friends that are friends we ought to see
You know, Bill and Ed and John and Frances and Mary
They seem slightly perplexed as to why we've come
And in the dark about exactly, just exactly what they can do for us.

What you need to get round this dilemma is a CV – not only for that particular interview but for that interviewer's contacts because a large part of the object of this contact-building exercise is to create a network of people working for you and listening for you until the network becomes dense enough to catch something. If you put yourself in the position of the person whom you are seeing for a moment, it becomes clear why you need to give some sort of formal picture of what you have to offer – even to people whom you think know you quite well. Supposing someone says to them, 'That person you told me about the other day – does he/she know anything about promoting furniture at the top end of the market?'. The chances are that your contact will not be able to answer the question and at best will say something like 'Well, I *think* so – I seem to remember he/she said they'd worked for "x" or it may have been "y". No, I can't remember exactly what he/she did but he's/she's always been on the marketing side.' A for effort but E for conviction.

It would all be much easier if your contact said, 'He/she gave me a CV – I'll send it off to you and ask them to get in touch.'

This kind of CV, however, is different from that which you would prepare in response to a specific advertisement because you want to leave as many options open as possible – without actually being vague about your achievements. It also ought to be shorter because it is going to someone who wants a brief resumé of your background not a detailed statement of how you meet a particular job specification. Government ministers often ask for what they call a 'position paper' from their civil servants – a document which sets out succinctly the background of a situation and indicates whether it is one they need to get involved with further. The contact CV has similar aims and should be a brief statement of:

– broad objectives (not a job title)
– experience
– qualifications

Here for instance is one for an executive who wants to move to a different career path:

Cyril Jones, 11 Uplands Road, London SW6 3TN
Telephone: 736 4992
Age: 33, married

Objectives: To expand my business experience by moving from personnel management and training to sales and marketing; preferably in the building products field. I would prefer not to drop significantly below my current earnings level of £14,000 per annum.[1]

Qualifications: I hold a CNAA degree in Business Studies. I have conducted courses and prepared a variety of training manuals for salesmen selling to a professional market. I converted my own holiday home in Shropshire over the last two years, conducting the entire building works myself. I am currently studying by correspondence for a further qualification in marketing.

Experience: I have worked in management and training since graduating in 1972. I am now in charge of in-company training for XYZ Limited at every level including the production of training manuals and videos. In the late 70s I represented the Personnel Department in an in-house consultancy exercise which devised a new incentive scheme. This produced a 30 per cent rise in productivity related to an overall wage rise of 12 per cent. Lately I have been engaged in computerising personnel records.

Some people might feel embarrassed about handling such a formal document to a friend, though even a friend might not have at his or her disposal the facts about you that are relevant to your job search. The best way to handle this problem – if you feel it to be a problem – is to ask them to advise you on your CV: are your objectives realistic in the light of what they know about you?

In fact, theirs will certainly be the best source of opinions about personal matters. Acquaintances will usually be less willing or qualified to talk honestly about your strengths or weaknesses – and should they do so, their opinions might be harder to take. Indeed, an important part of the process of thinking about 'how' your contact can help you is to turn the question around again and ask 'what' they can help you with. A former colleague occupying a middle management position cannot realistically be expected to come up with much information above the level at which he operates. A person in another function than the one you have targeted is unlikely to do more than give you an introduction to someone who is nearer the bullseye. A real blue-chip top-level contact will probably only have a general overview of the job scene rather than being in a position to give you specific leads – but his name might work wonders in terms of introductions. That at least is the position you start out with; how you develop it is a skill which career consultants tell you is something you will learn as your experience of contact interviews builds up.

Setting Up Contact Interviews

All the authorities that have written or spoken about the job-hunting process stress that it is incredibly hard work, though you can make it even harder for yourself and more discouraging to boot by joining the ranks of those who send out hundreds of round-Robin letters without getting a single interview (in this area at least the law of averages does not seem to hold true). Getting contact interviews does require a lot of research, a lot of legwork and the labour of preparing letters aimed at individuals; but it does work.

Why should this be so? Why should anyone want to see you when as far as you know they may not actually be looking for someone at all? One reason is because organisations are never static. They are never without some problem somewhere. 'Every company', says Minster's Jack Barnes, 'has opportunities that they are throwing away because there is no-one there to exploit them'. Similarly every company has long-term plans for expansion even though they are still vague ones, and every company has

Jobs in a Jobless World

someone somewhere who is not 'working out' in the position they are in. The attraction of the contact interview from a company's point of view is that it offers the chance of a stress-free meeting where they can measure up a possible contender without any commitment being asked for or offered. This is why it is essential not to raise the question of a job either directly or indirectly at any time before, during or after the meeting. Once you do that the spell is broken and the person at the other end gets to feel like the window-shopper who is being pressed to buy when all he wanted to do was look.

On the other hand, no busy executive wants to see you just to 'chew the fat' in the American phrase. In some way your initial letter must address itself to his or her wants and this is where your research and the information you have gleaned in other contact interviews comes into play – not necessarily overtly but certainly by implication. The moment you make it overt you are in the dangerous position of – apparently – asking for a job. So you do not write 'I hear you are thinking of setting up a research laboratory in applied physical chemistry' but you dangle the bait:

It may interest you to know that I am deputy head of one of the major research divisions at British Glue Products Limited with a staff of forty graduates and that my job has involved close liaison with the marketing division, particularly in relation to the development of 'Gelatigen' which, as you know, is now widely used in many convenience foods.

Fuller details of what you want and what you have to offer should be kept for your CV. The letter is a bare-bones document which:

- states who referred you to the person you are writing to
- points out the specific thing in your CV which might interest him or her
- says briefly what you have to offer in relation to what you believe is their most immediate need
- suggests a meeting (on this there are two school of thought – those who say that you should indicate that you will phone to set up a meeting and those who

maintain that you should merely say you are available for interview and look forward to hearing further. Which you choose must depend on how hard you think you are going to have to sell yourself.)

Much of this becomes more difficult in the case of the 'blind' contact interview. Without a referral you have to work even harder on your research to find out a point of contact between the company's needs and what you have to offer; because unless you can establish this almost at first glance, your letter is likely to land up straight in the waste-paper basket. This is mostly going to happen anyway, one has to say, if you do not go beyond the *Times 1,000* list of biggest companies. Smaller firms are a better bet but even there the risk of being screened out if you come without an introduction is high. Some rules for avoiding this fate are:

- never write to the Personnel Manager (unless you want a job in Personnel, of course). Personnel do not initiate hiring decisions outside their own department even though they are used as experts in the hiring process
- always find out the name and initials of the person who can make the hiring decision in your sphere and at your level. Quite often the switchboard will tell you if you have no other means of getting it. If someone asks, 'What is it in connection with?' (a favourite telephonist's or secretary's ploy for parrying unwanted callers), say that it is a confidential matter. If you sound confident enough, that will usually do the trick.
- mark your letter CONFIDENTIAL. That way it will generally go on the desk of the person to whom it is addressed; and, after all, anything to do with possible staff or policy matters legitimately falls into this category.
- If you possibly can, lead off your letter with an item of interest to the person you are addressing, either because it is relevant to their company needs or because it is something they have said or written. Few things are sweeter or more flattering than the sound of applause or even the sign that someone has taken notice of something you have said. One would be prepared to bet, for instance, that a letter to the

chairman of the house-building firm which was written up in *Campaign*, would have produced a response.

Never be trapped into conducting an interview on the phone. For some reason – maybe because a certain amount of rapport can only be established face to face – it never works.

The Contact Interview

How are you going to conduct an interview which does not have filling a job as its primary objective? This is an important question to sort out in your mind because nothing is more embarrassing than for the dialogue to falter and die; and it can easily happen if the person you are seeing is not a good conversationalist and if you have not done your homework. Many a promising meeting has petered out within the first five minutes on the words, 'Well, we don't actually have anything for you, Mr, Ms er . . .' The problem here is that both parties are thinking along conventional lines.

They think that, in spite of declaration to the contrary, you want a job.

You, in spite of declaration to the contrary, are aghast that they have not offered you one.

End of further useful discussion. What a pity because what you are really after is a definition of your problem and a rearrangement of the facts relating to it. Ultimately you might highlight a problem *the interviewer* has, and it may not even happen then but weeks or months later when he or she remembers your meeting. Right now, though, the issue is to keep the ball in the air. All you are after is information and the fact that there is no job in the offing is not important. That is the end of the process, not its beginning.

Conversations are infinitely varied in their progress and to try to give rules for conducting them would be a waste of time. Some consultants do suggest that you should take a good look around the interviewer's room because it can give you some clues to his or her tastes. If you are fortunate enough to find someone who is interested in the same things as you are, that obviously does give you a point of contact. But in most cases what most people in the inter-viewer/interviewee relationship have in common is shop; and of course in a contact meeting they have in common the person who provided the referral. Thus you might start off by talking about the mutual acquaintance who affected the introduction: how he is doing, what business is like, what his problems are. Let us take this process a little further and at the risk of seeming to set out an interview formula – an impossible task – let us at any rate suggest a typical course for the dialogue in a meeting of this kind to take:

INTERVIEWEE: Well, one of the really interesting things Perkins told me was that AB Co. were missing out badly in the widget market in the USA. They are doing quite well in Europe, apparently, but manufacturers are desperate for the things in America and unless AB Co. get their skates on, someone out East will simply produce a cheaper version.

CONTACT: No, I hadn't heard that . . . AB Co. are doing well in Europe, are they? Our market share has been down lately and of course our product coexists with theirs. That must mean some competitor is moving in. I must give Perkins a ring and see what he knows about it.

INTERVIEWEE: Do you know anyone I could talk to about AB Co.? I have had quite a lot of experience in the widget field – haven't done much lately but I could pick up the threads again – and of course as you will have seen from my CV I do know the East quite well and I would be in a good position to negotiate manufacturer licenses out there.

CONTACT: Yes, so I see . . . No, I don't really know anyone at AB Co. but I believe Jones does. He is the Production Director at DEF Co. He knows quite a lot about their product. They've just introduced that new computerised widget of theirs and they are pretty enthusiastic about it, though they've found they have to tinker with the programmes of some of the things they're doing. He reckons that if AB Co. developed some more applications packages they would have a real winner . . .

I'll tell you want, though, I think Smith at British Carbon Fibres would be very interested in knowing something about the research you have been doing. What sort of results are you getting?

INTERVIEWEE: Well, We've been getting some fantastic fuel savings on long-haul flights but there are a lot of teething troubles. Engine wear has been a problem.

CONTACT: I don't think Smith is quite in the same field but I have heard he's not entirely happy with his R and D people.

INTERVIEWEE: Do you think it is worth sending them my CV?

CONTACT: Definitely.

INTERVIEWEE: May I ask you what you think of it? I'd obviously re-write it if I send it in to Smith but is there anything I should change?

CONTACT: Well, I would certainly go into more detail about what you have been doing at Fuel Control Monitoring. Why do you want to leave them, by the way? You seem to be doing all right there.

INTERVIEWEE: Well, the problem is that with the slump in airlines in the last couple of years, FCM have been finding things a bit sticky. I have heard on the grapevine that there is a serious possibility that my division might be closed down so I thought I would start looking round.

CONTACT: Sensible move. Well, BCF aren't really in that part of the market, as I said. Smith is a pretty canny fellow – got an MBA at Harvard, you know – and he saw the whole airline problem coming. They are more in the industrial application end of things now. All his directors were against it but he's a bit of an autocrat.

INTERVIEWEE: My problem would be that I don't know too much about the industrial applications. Is there anyone who might be able to give me some background?

CONTACT: Well, there's old Bill Patterson who's just retired from BCF – he and Smith didn't see eye to eye, I should warn you, but he knows most of the people in the business, etc. etc.

Not all contacts, one has to admit, are going to be as forthcoming as this. Almost as disconcerting as the I-don't-think-we-have-any-job-at-the-moment response is the comment when you ask for further referrals who can help you augment your knowledge of a particular industry or firm, 'No, I don't think I know anyone'. In that case you have to use your judgment whether you have struck a really awkward customer, someone you have simply not hit it off with, or someone who, given a few days to think it over, might come up with a name. The first two are actually rarer in this type of interview than in some job interviews because in general when you do get a referral your primary contact will in the nature of things refer you to an individual you are likely to get on with. If you are a member of a minority group, for instance, he or she may not refer you to a fellow member of it but they certainly won't put you on to someone with a violent prejudice against it.

On the other hand, even a sticky interview is good practice for the real thing. Indeed, one of the many virtues of the contact interview, and one of the reasons why career counsellors are so keen on them, is this aspect because, as we have already explained, you will not get enough actual job interviews to use them to polish your techniques or to cope with awkward questions and situations. You will have noticed, for instance, in our imaginary script, that the contact raised the question, 'Why do you want to leave?'. The truth of the matter may well be that the interviewee knows full well that he is going to be made redundant or even that he has had a thundering row with his present boss. It is a question that often throws candidates in an actual interview into a lather of embarrassment, explanation or recrimination – all of them fatal to their chances – but in a contact interview you learn to field it neatly.

Apart from that, you will notice, this type of interview fills several other purposes. One, of course, is to get referrals to yet more people who will help you fill in the job picture. You will notice also that the interviewee not only does not ask for a job – he does not even ask for a referral to a contact who will give him a job; though, interestingly enough, the contact does immediately start trying to think of someone at AB Co. even though he cannot actually come up with a name. What he does do (prompted incidentally by a smart but handy piece of knowledge which the interviewee has relayed to *him*) is to disclose a great deal of useful background information about companies that the interviewee might get in touch with – what they do and what their problems are and in one case what their chief executive is like. No doubt Bill Patterson, the recently retired director, will come up with a great deal more information so that when the interviewee does finally get to see Smith he may well have spotted the unadvertised slot that he could fill; at least by that time he will have acquired an understanding of the problems and opportunities facing BCF that is bound to impress the people there. What can happen now is well described by Ted Simpson of Saunders & Sydney:

> At some point the guy you are seeing is going to start moving into a different gear. He sits up in his chair. His questions are going to become more and more direct and pointed. He buzzes his secretary and tells her to take his calls for the time being. He starts focusing on your CV. He asks where you can be reached. He asks, 'Do you mind if I call in X or Y – I think they would be very interested in what you are telling me'. He says, 'Are you free for lunch next week? – I would like you to go into more detail about this or that.' Or, 'I would like you to meet our Finance Director – when are you free?.' (Never say 'Anytime', by the way – make it look as though you are in demand.) In other words, you have got lift-off.

Sometimes, though rarely, a meeting of this kind produces an actual job offer. The universal advice in that case is to play it cool. Again, you don't want to give the impression that you are not a chooser – and, by implication, a beggar. Ask to be told more about the position they have in mind and even have a couple of days to think it over. As soon as you get home, write a letter confirming that the offer has been made, and say you will call to have a meeting to discuss it; while in the meantime sorting out in your own mind exactly what you want to pitch for. Sometimes, though, rarely, the offer will not be confirmed. There are impulsive executives who, after an ample lunch, make offers they regret by late afternoon. Not working for someone like that may not be a matter for enduring regret.

More likely, obviously, is that you will walk out with nothing more substantial than some additional interview experience, a few names of further people to see and an addition to your fund of knowledge; or so it seems. The fact is, though, that an idea takes some while to germinate and maybe at some time a job possibility will be mooted with one of the firms you have contacted. Thus self-interest as well as good manners dictate that you should always send a thank-you note after every interview no matter how useless you feel it has been. Nothing long or fulsome; a simple note of thanks with some reference to what you found most useful about the meeting will do. Those who have been pleasant to you will appreciate it, those who have not will at least feel guilty.

---

[1] Some consultants advise against mentioning salaries at all until a job offer has been made. On the other hand, if you have a broad salary objective the contact interviewer who, it can be remembered, is not the job interviewer, will find it helpful to know what bracket you are aiming at.

11. The Interview Game and How to Win It

A job interview is a form of examination and like an examination it is in many ways a very imperfect method of judging ability. But in an examination you at least have several papers and usually many hours in which to demonstrate what is often criticised as being memory as much as knowledge. A job interview gives you a great deal less time in which to put over a much more complex message. You have to convince someone, on what evidence of past performance you can muster, plus the way you project your personality, that you are able to handle not only the job itself but the relationships that go with it. Furthermore, although in an examination there are many gradations between passing with distinction and failure, in a job interview there are only absolutes; you either go to the next stage, that is to the short list or the job itself, or you fail.

That is an alarming prospect for the interviewee, but it is hardly less so for the interviewer. A professional – a consultant working on behalf of a client or an in-house personnel specialist selecting a short list for a line manager – has the benefit of experience and skill at asking questions that produce revealing answers. He is also in the comforting position of not actually having to make the really big decision – all he or she has to do (in the interests of simplicity we will use a unisex 'he' for the rest of this chapter) is to submit a list of candidates. Some of them may be choices that the ultimate employer does not agree with, but provided that the consultant or personnel manager does not make a habit of submitting short lists with too high a proportion of duds, his fee or salary is safe.

The person who actually has to make the appointment has no such option. He only has one choice and he has to live with it, even though out of the whole chain of people along which the candidate has to pass, he is often the one least skilled and experienced in the art of interviewing. He is also the one who pays most dearly if he makes a mistake. A consultant's judgment may be called into question over the choice of a short-listed candidate, but for the employer a mistake may be a disaster which can ultimately rock his own position. At the very least it will cost a lot of money. It takes several months to spot even fairly gross incompetence and to grasp the nettle of the consequences. Then there is usually some form of compensation to be paid out and a further period before a replacement is found who may take months to sort out the mess. The whole exercise seldom costs less than a year's salary. As the writer of *What Color Is Your Parachute?* neatly puts it:

> In one twenty-minute interview, the man with the power to hire can botch up part of the organisation, cost the organisation a great deal of money, lose his own promotion, be called to account and acquire a whole new set of ulcers. No wonder hiring is such a stressful situation.

A variety of additional selection methods are sometimes used to bring some degree of scientific accuracy and predictability to this alarmingly hit or miss business. Some continental countries are very keen on graphology. American companies, in particular, often favour intelligence, aptitude or personality tests in addition to interviews. They have never really caught on in the UK, perhaps because, like telephone tapping, they are thought to be unfair. The chief British variant on the theme of the one-to-one interview is the selection panel – selection by committee, in other words – but on the whole what interviewers go by is simply whether or not they like the candidate. Even when headhunters or selection consultants are employed as job brokers, in the final analysis they rely enormously not only on whether candidates fulfil the job description but whether they think the client will 'get on' with him and vice versa. It is a theme that crops up again and again in answer to the question put to a wide variety of employers and job brokers on what finally determines their choice. The whole situation is perfectly summed up by Anthony Jay in his book *Corporation Man*. He begins by questioning the value of interviews on the grounds that:

Under the cloak of a dispassionate appraisal by question and answer, irrational judgments are being made on the basis of qualities which are not mentioned in the job description.

He goes on to describe how personnel specialists have tried to put the process on a more scientific footing but he then, with agreeable and illuminating candour, goes on to tell of his own experience as a manager responsible for making hiring decisions:

When I first reached a managerial position in which I had to appoint people to vacancies, I was convinced that one of the greatest barriers to corporation justice was the selection of people for jobs on the grounds (probably never admitted) that the interviewer liked them. I was determined that I at least would always pick the best candidate irrespective of any irrelevant personal feelings. That resolution fell at the first fence. My very first vacancy produced a candidate who by any objective measurement was noticeably better than the others, but I just could not see myself working with him without a harsh, grating sensation somewhere in the region of my colon. Nor could I see any of the rest of the team taking to him. There was nothing in the needs of the job or in his qualifications to exclude him, but all the same it simply was not possible for me to appoint him. At the time I thought that my resolution had weakened unforgivably, and I had better abandon any hopes of being a modern scientific manager. I now realize that wisdom had triumphed over intellect.

The revelation – if revelation it is – that success or failure in an interview depends on something as primitive as gut feeling, might prompt some candidates simply to leave it all to fate, personal chemistry or whatever mystery governs the establishment of a rapport with another person. But it is not as uncontrollable as that. An interview is a social transaction which goes through several stages and there are many interviewer's reports which begin, 'I did /didn't greatly take to this candidate at first glance but then I dug deeper . . .'. In other words, an initial impression is capable of being modified one way or the other in the course taken by the rest of the encounter.

First Impressions

That initial impression is, however, made and it is amazing how often people handicap themselves unnecessarily right from the start. A recent survey shows that one in four people turn up late for interviews (quite a number never turn up at all) and though it was taken from a poll across the whole job scene, a great many applicants for professional and managerial jobs mar their chances in this way. Whether the situation can be retrieved by a tactic suggested by one career consultant, who recommends that if you are late you should not embark on long excuses or explanations but simply say, 'I am sorry I am late – I won't bore you with the details', is very doubtful. It depends on how strong your case is in other respects but even if you get away with it, few people are at their best arriving hot, bothered and having parked on a double yellow line or in the chairman's reserved bay. Therefore, in making preparations for the interview, you should not neglect the obvious ones of finding out exactly where you have to get to and how long it takes to get there. If you arrive reasonably early, it will leave you time to check over the points you want to bring out in your CV or application form against the job specification, to give yourself a last-minute brief on the employer, to note the surroundings, take in the atmosphere and maybe look in a few estate agents' windows to get an idea of house prices. You can also go back over your own list of questions because you should try to memorise them. A lot of interviewers are put off by candidates who bring out sheaves of written notes like a speaker about to embark on a long, boring discourse.

Some of this may sound superfluous but interviewers are full of stories of candidates who start off on every known variant of the wrong foot, of which the most common are scruffiness, blatant signs of nervousness or anxiety and smoking heavily when the interviewer, from the absence of an ashtray, is clearly a non-smoker. There are even cases, by no means as unusual as one might think, of candidates who have made the absolutely fatal error of having fortified themselves with one glass too many.

Below this level it becomes rather more difficult to give advice because one does enter the realms of simple and often idiotic prejudice against various expressions of individuality in dress or appearance. On the whole you would be well advised to conform to what is generally regarded as the 'uniform' of the profession or occupation. Thus a flamboyant accountant might be regarded with as much suspicion as a designer in a conservative three-piece suit of undistinguished cut. Bear in mind the instructive, though presumably apocryphal story of the officer who was court-martialled for chasing a lady down a hotel corridor dressed only in his uniform jacket. He was cleared on the grounds that he was properly dressed for the occupation in which he was engaged.

The question this raises is to what extent you should hide your nature in order to make a good impression. Certainly there is a school of thought which believes you should not try to do this. Talking of younger applicants, one personnel officer stressed that he wanted to see them as they are, not as their parents thought they ought to present themselves because nobody's interests were served if he took on someone under the wrong impression. This view is echoed by Piers Wemyss who, speaking of more senior interviewees, says:

> It is very doubtful whether it is in your interests or those of an employer to put on an act. It's a bit like cramming for an exam. You may pass the exam but if you are basically not very bright or unsuited to the profession in which you have qualified, it does not do anybody much good.

All this, however, is a matter of degree. Every situation where you have to interact with others requires some degree of conformity and in the course of the interview what you have to determine, just as much as the interviewer, is whether you think you will fit in; in other words, whether the extent and kind of conformity required is one you think you can live with. This is something younger job seekers, less sure of themselves, still testing basic assumptions about themselves, as we indicated in Chapter 4, sometimes find it very difficult to accept. The only words of advice one can give is that if you want a job you will not be able to stick out as an oddball in the interview and that to conform does not make you a conformist. The American astronauts, for instance, who seemed to conform absolutely to a norm of clean, God-fearing, white Anglo-Saxon Protestant virtue, turned out to be a much odder bunch when the journalist Tom Wolfe wrote about them in his ironically titled book *The Right Stuff*. As Wolfe showed, they had to suppress their individuality to fit the image the US Air Force projected of them.

But whereas it is relatively easy to do something about the impression one makes intentionally on other people, it is far more difficult to do something about the unintentional ones. In a poem entitled – inappropriately, one hopes – 'To A Louse' – Robert Burns wrote:

> Oh wad some Power the giftie gie us
> To see oursels as others see us,
> It wad from many a blunder free us
> And foolish notion.

Here, however, the new technology has come to our aid and most career consultants now use video recordings to train clients in interview techniques. Some recruiters are worried about this because it does smack of what might be called personality face-lifting and certainly it would be a mistake to use it for that end, if indeed this is possible. However, as a method of eliminating broad-brush errors of personal presentation, it has been found to be helpful. If you believe empathy goes beyond crude personal chemistry to its definition in Chambers Dictionary: 'The power of entering into another's personality and imaginatively experiencing his experience', then the ability to see yourself in purely physical terms as others see you is an important first stage in that direction.

Reassuring the Interviewer

Some twenty years ago, the psychologist Hans Eysenck had this to say about job interviews:

> We must conclude that the interview is almost a complete failure and the time devoted to it as far as prediction (of performance) is concerned goes wasted.

Nevertheless, it is still about the only method we have of choosing people for jobs, so recruiters are naturally worried that if candidates learn interview techniques it will reduce the value of the interview as selection tool still further. Not so; because to have made sensible preparation for being interviewed does, in fact, demonstrate many of the qualities the interviewer should be looking for. He should beware far more of the candidates who have not prepared themselves properly.

But apart from question spotting – a topic we will turn to later – what other preparations can you make? Once again it turns on the question of empathy – putting yourself in the other person's shoes. The interviewer has problems too. By the time he sees you he has done the easy bit which is to say 'no' to 90 per cent of the applicants, assuming the vacancy is an advertised one. Nobody is going to tax him with turning anyone down unless he has accidentally rejected a highly qualified friend of the boss's (he would probably have gone the unadvertised route anyway). What they *will* tax him with is if he recommends or appoints the wrong person, even though he has little information on that person and less evidence to support it. All he has to go on when he goes into the interview is the candidate's CV, application form or letter. After that he has to rely on his own experience, skill and judgment. So what he is looking for is reassurance that he is making the right decision. The candidate who understands that and who empathises with the interviewer's dilemma, is *much* more likely to be successful than the one who is merely preoccupied with getting a job.

One reason for this is that he will have thought about the points where the interviewer is looking for reassurance. In the words of another American best-seller on job-hunting, *Guerilla Tactics in the Job Market*:

The employer is waiting to hear a simple, positive statement from the candidate which expresses clearly what the employer is looking for. The message is really not as involved and complex as most job-seekers think. It is simply the answer to the generally inarticulated question, 'Why should I hire you?'. This is the underlying context of the interview which the candidate must satisfy.

It would be hard to improve on this statement except to say that the employer wants reassurance on a whole series of matters. Firstly, he wants you to demonstrate that you understand the requirements of the job and that does not only mean that you have read the job description but that you have some grasp of the organisation and its problems. Here are some things you should check on before you go for an interview:

- What products or services does the employer supply? – not only those in your immediate area of interest.
- What is their reputation for quality, delivery, etc.?
- How do they compare with the competition?
- What are the problems of the industry, trade or profession in general?
- What specific problems has the firm or industry as a whole had to face lately, or is likely to face in the future?
- What have you done in a similar situation?
- What points in your CV or application are likely to worry/attract the interviewer in relation to the job?

The second set of things on which you have to reassure him is a much less tangible one – that of character. Every employer has had experience of the person, well qualified on paper and in terms of experience, who turns out to be lacking in more abstract but essential attributes such as energy, motivation, initiative, leadership, the ability to work with others or whatever skills and virtues the job may call for. Reassurance in this regard can only be a question of relating your achievements to qualities such as these. For instance, the American Management Association recently identified a number of characteristics required for senior jobs but in fact they fit almost any kind of professional or executive position including junior ones:

- Ability to initiate action
- Skill in arranging events into a causal sequence
- Assembling data into new, meaningful patterns
- Free, easy self-expression
- Ability to be objective about two sides of an argument
- Placing organisational above personal needs
- Ability to work hard, adapt, to be flexible
- Satisfaction in actions that will help others
- Ability to gain compliance of others
- Ability to make effective presentations
- Ability to stimulate teamwork

Younger job seekers, particularly those with limited work experience, might think that they would be hard put to it to demonstrate such qualities as these but there again it is a matter of offering reassurance in a way that is appropriate to the situation. No employer expects to see a ready-made young executive leaping into the interview room – indeed, some would be appalled by the prospect – but as one young man says:

> Employers look avidly for any signs of initiative or enterprise. If on the dole, volunteer for charity work, for instance. Any activity that puts the candidate out of the ordinary will dramatically improve his or her chances and if you have a particular career in mind, do everything possible to become more acquainted with it. A friend of mine who wants to get into film-making is driving a truck for a video hire company and using the time to become familiar with the equipment. Applicants with no work experience can only offer the employer a hope of success. Those who have some achievement, some work experience, even if it is limited, will improve their chances enormously.

To some degree, therefore, any kind of interviewer's questions will be an attempt to establish the right mix of practical experience and personal qualities and relate them to the job. The skill with which this is done, the extent to which the procedures are formalised, and the areas in your CV or application which they will centre on depend not only on the interviewer but on the type of interview. You should therefore make your preparations accordingly as far as you can. The recruitment consultant's or personnel department's job interview will be different from one conducted by a headhunter and both will be different from that of the line manager making an actual appointment.

Types of Interview

The recruitment consultant or personnel department, having eliminated 90 per cent of the applicants on the basis of their initial response, is now concerned to eliminate still further. Some consultants specialise in specific industries or functional areas but as a rule this type of interview will not be concerned with details of technical competence as much as gaining a personal impression of applicants whose response will have suggested they ought to be seen, and to test them further on the extent to which they match up to the job description. Some interviewers have highly formalised procedures for doing this; one that is quoted in many books for interviewers and personnel managers is the sevenpoint plan devised by Professor Alec Rodger. This identifies every job as calling for certain attributes, some related to specific skills and some concerned with character:

- physical makeup (i.e. appearance)
- attainment
- general intelligence
- special aptitudes
- interests
- disposition
- personal circumstances

It suggests that the job specification should be analysed in these terms and the applicants rated accordingly. Like a lot of forms of assessment, Rodgers's seven-point plan is simply a form of applied commonsense and every professionally conducted interview will bring these aspects into play even if it is a 'biographical' one where the interviewer goes through your CV, probing sensitive spots with varying degrees of delicacy.

This may seem to put the interviewee into a somewhat passive role where it is difficult to make a positive impression – and easy to make a negative one. The best way to deal with it is through the quality of the questions *you* ask about the employer, whose identity will normally be revealed at an early stage: his policies, problems, plans and reporting structure. As we said earlier, technical questions do not come into this, and one should beware of annoying the interviewer by blinding him with science. On the other hand, one experienced recruiter did suggest that it is a good idea to take advantage of the screening interviewer's lack of specific technical knowledge by dropping in just a few technical questions. If they are tactfully put (that is, not with the patent intention of catching him out), intelligent and troubling, and he is not able to answer them, he may feel duty bound to refer you to someone who can; in this case the line manager who sees the short list.

The headhunter's interview will, of course, be quite different. In this case it is *he* who has done the research. As we showed in the chapter on job brokers, he will have found out on your behalf a great deal about the client company's needs, problems and general atmosphere. He will also have found out quite a lot about *you* through various sources. As one headhunter's proposal to clients puts it, they look for industries where suitable candidates can be found, then for successful companies within those industries and finally zero in on successful individuals within those companies who meet the job specification. The object of the headhunter's interview, therefore, is not so much to establish whether you are good enough – though no doubt there will be some discreet probing as to whether you are as good as your no doubt glowing recommendations suggest – but whether the job is in accord with your personal goals in terms of career objectives, job satisfaction and living and working environments at this juncture; and whether the personal chemistry between you and the headhunter's client will work. It is in these areas, therefore, as well as in those of the contents of the job itself, that your questions should be pitched. This type of interview, incidentally, will be much longer than a recruitment consultant's one, if only for the reason that high salaries and major jobs are usually involved.

Panel interviews are a form of interviewing by committee. It has been said of committees that they are a substitute for the agony of thought and the loneliness of decision and an organisation that interviews by this method may indicate that it lacks a strong leader. On the other hand, where you are being asked to join a team, it may well be that the people whom you will be working with expect to be consulted and this could be a growing trend in high-skill, high technology firms where hierarchies are much less rigid than in more established organisations. The vote of every person in the panel counts, at least in theory, and it is therefore important to make each of them think you are giving them your attention. Unfortunately this is quite often difficult to do. One member, more aggressive, more intelligent, or quite often more boring and self-important than the others, will try to hog the limelight. The trick is to answer his questions while remaining in eye contact with, and in mute appeal to, the others to give them a chance to chip in. Equally dangerous is the temptation to get involved in long technical discussions with one particular member of the panel which interest him and you but not the others. You should also be alert to the presence of the real decision-maker if there is one. He may not be as obvious as the leader of the vervet monkeys described in *Corporation Man*:

> The status of adult males in the troop is demonstrated by the colour of the scrotum – deepest indigo is number one, shading down to the palest pastel blue for the monkey at the bottom of the heap.

In the absence of such signs, it is a question of being sensitive to the situation. There is usually something in the atmosphere, something in the way people react and defer to one member of the company which indicates he is the boss.

Where you are required to work as part of a team, selection may also be based wholly or in part on your performance in a *group interview*. One of British Airways's selection tests for cabin crew was described by Trevor Austin, BA's manager of employment services, as follows:

> Cabin crew candidates are brought into a room as a group of eight. The room has a table on which there is some paper, sticky tape and scissors. The chairs are uncomfortable and much lower than the table. The group is invited to construct a paper tower. This task simulates a cabin crew situation when a group of people who often have not worked before have to complete a variety of tasks in rather uncomfortable circumstances. The interviewing panel look out for who emerges as a leader, as the person who has the ideas, who mucks in, who fools about, and so forth.

Other tests of this kind are based on group discussions. The short-listed candidates are given a topic to discuss while observers from the employers or the consultants sit in the background taking notes of what goes on and what reaction you have on other members of the group. The observers are interested in how well you marshal your facts, how articulate you are in putting them over and how quick you are in thinking on your feet. Like a good team games player, though, you should avoid running selfishly with the ball even if you are a brilliant solo performer. A well-timed pass to another player can often be more impressive than a dazzling individual effort. It will make you more popular with the rest of the group, too. The main thing, though, is to say *something*, preferably something intelligent, at a fairly early stage, partly because it will encourage others to come back at you, thereby keeping you in the discussion, and partly because it will give you confidence to go on.

There is no such interview type as the *line manager's interview*. But clearly at some point you will come face to face with the person who actually makes the hiring decision. He will usually be the most stressed and least expert of all the people you meet. If he has done a lot of interviewing in his time he may have a set and logical routine – the usual one is to tell you about the job and the organisation, to ask you questions designed to test your claims, expertise and attitudes and finally to invite *you* to ask *him* questions. On the other hand, he might have no set plan at all and simply thrash around your CV doing most of the talking himself and hoping you will come up with something. The best kind of interview is a conversation and if your interviewer is awkward and untrained, the best plan is to put him at ease by getting him on to the subject of shop as soon as possible. Ultimately, though, the real trouble with interviews is that there are no rules to follow except for the golden oldie 'Don't knock your current or previous employer in any way, no matter how much you loathe him.' Attempts to establish rules are apt to end up like an article in a national newspaper on being interviewed which, though otherwise sensible, said: 'Don't stare your interviewer in the eye, look at the end of his nose.' It would be hard to think which is more disconcerting. The best advice has been given by a very experience personnel man turned senior line manager who, when asked about the subject, said:

> What interviewers really look for is some evidence that the candidate has done his or her homework and is able to discuss the company and its products intelligently. But grilling the interviewer and telling him what is wrong with his organisation is not popular either.

Ultimately the only law in interviewing is what the American writer May Parker Follett calls 'the law of the situation': a sensitivity for the atmosphere and for the people concerned.

Interview Questions and How to Deal With Them

You cannot predict the course of a human encounter such as an interview, which is one reason why consultants are chary of purely mechanical training in interview techniques. On the other hand, as we said earlier, an interview is like an exam and you can spot questions in the reasonable expectation that at least some of them will come up. Here are some questions which experienced consultants have found often to recur in interviews together with some ideas and possible answers which, corny though some of them may sound, are what the majority of interviewers like to hear:

'Why did you apply for the job?'

'Because I have always been interested in . . . since my experience of . . . and because everyone has told me that this is a good company to work for.'

'What are your strong points?'

(A very common question) Make your answer relate as much as possible to the qualities the job calls for and be able to prove them. Avoid vague answers such as you are good at dealing with people.

'What are your worst points?'

(Another common question) Awful though it may sound, never admit to real ones. Don't say you have none but don't make them sound serious. For instance if you are bad at judging people, say something to the effect that you expect too much of them.

'You must have been looking for quite a long time. Why do you think you are having trouble getting a job?'

'I don't want to rush at the first job on offer. I have simply taken time to find out as much as possible about the employers I am really interested in.'

'What do you look for in a job?'

Avoid hackneyed phrases like 'challenge', 'job satisfaction'. 'The opportunity to try out new ideas' is a better answer.

'What did you learn from your last job?'

Think of as much as possible that is relevant to the job you are now being interviewed for.

'You seem to have moved around a lot. Why is that?'

A difficult one. The best answer is to say that with the wisdom of hindsight it wasn't a good idea but at the time it seemed like a better way of getting all-round experience than sitting in one job for a long time.

'You seem to have stayed in your present/last job a long time. Why is that?'

Staying in a job too long is almost as bad as moving around too much – the best answer is to say that you thoroughly enjoyed the job and liked the people and that these were the most important factors as far as you were concerned.

'Why were you made redundant?'

A question which when relevant is always implied but not always asked. Some consultants suggest, in fact, that you should bring it out into the open to clear the air. The answer is, if at all tenable, that you could have stayed on in a sinecure but you didn't feel that was good either for the company or for yourself.

'What were your problems in your last job?'

Never run down your last employer. Build your answer round the idea that there weren't the resources to do everything that you wanted to. Try and concentrate on problems that you solved, not those that floored you.

'What do you think you could have done better?'
Nobody is perfect. Try and find something for which you were not profoundly to blame. 'I think if I could have foreseen how long the recession would last . . .'

'What do you know about us?'
A great opportunity for those who have done their homework, but don't overdo it. Try and make some intelligent comment rather than just reeling off lists of products.

'We have a problem with . . . How would you tackle it?'
This is not a trick question but one you have to be very careful with because you will not have the facts at your disposal. Answer it obliquely by showing how you previously dealt with a similar situation even if you have to make one up. Otherwise your answer may either be wrong or appear to be critical of the interviewer's firm.

'What would be your ideal job?'
It would be too obvious and corny to describe the one you are applying for. Describe some of its characteristics plus others you have enjoyed elsewhere.

'What took your notice in today's paper?'
A question often put to younger job seekers. Pick out and think about some item in the quality dailies before your interview.

163

'Are you considering any other offers?'

If you have had one, mention it. If not, say you have been concentrating on this one because it is the job you most want to do.

'If your present employer made you a better offer, would you accept it?'

'Every man has his price, but on the whole I feel ready to make a move.'

'Where do you expect to be in three years' time?'

A common question. A good answer would be that job titles are not important to you but that you expect to have fulfilled the major objectives of the job being advertised. Avoid unrealistic goals that could brand you as a dreamer.

'What do you think was your major achievement in your last job?'

Something that relates to the requirements of the present one. Try and give credit to others for their contribution while making it clear that you were the prime mover.

'You seem to have little experience in . . . (some ingredient of the job). How would you get round that?'

Don't say it would be no problem; that is too facile. Mention some area in a previous job where you had no experience but overcame the hurdle successfully; or offer to undergo training in your own time. It will probably not be an essential part of the job, otherwise they would not have asked you to come for an interview.

'How did you get your last job?'

The best answer is that you were recommended to the employer by a third party. In the case of younger job seekers, some evidence of personal initiative is most telling in your favour.

'What do you do in your spare time?'

The best answer depends tremendously on the type of job and what you have been able to guess about the employer. There is a good deal of prejudice in some quarters against intellectual pursuits, for instance. Beware also of mentioning pursuits that are very time consuming, like politics. The reaction to your answer will tell you a lot about your potential employer anyway.

'Don't you feel you are a bit young for the job?'

'I have moved up rather quickly so far, I agree, but I have never had any problem about handling older people under me.'

'Don't you feel you are a bit old for the job?'

'Well, I agree I could handle a wider range of tasks and responsibilities. For instance, it seems to me . . . ' This is where you bring your study of the organisation's needs and problems to bear and show what further contribution you can make.

'What have you been doing with yourself since your last employment?'

Quite a number of employers look very kindly on people who have taken on temporary work – particuarly in the case of recent graduates and school leavers.

'What do your sub-ordinates/colleagues think of you?'

Mention good points; bad ones should not be fatal drawbacks. Impatience, for instance, is a fairly harmless vice that some might even consider to be

	a virtue: so is being a perfectionist.
(To women applicants) 'What happens if you get married?'	'I am not planning to but if I did it would not interfere with my work.'
(To married women applicants) 'What happens if you start a family?'	'I am not planning to but if I did you would get at least six months' notice – which is more than most people give.'
'If we were to offer you a job, when could you start?'	For a person out of work this is no problem. In work you are normally obliged to give about three months' notice and the chances are the new employer wants you to start sooner than that. However, it creates a bad impression if you are prepared to leave the old one in the lurch. 'I am on three months' notice so I will have to consult with the people I am working for. I think they would probably let me go after six weeks provided I agree to pop in for six weeks after that to help my successor.'

Giving specimen answers like this is treading on dangerous ground and it would be self-defeating if every reader of this book rehearsed them. On the other hand they do illustrate an underlying principle which is worth remembering: every question has a purpose which is to find out something about your circumstances, your achievements, your attitudes, or other things about you that bother the interviewer. Though the questions tend to be predictable, the right way to answer them is not to come up with a pat reply, but to consider why they have been asked. For instance, an interviewer probably would ask an attractive unmarried woman about what would happen if her status were to change. The reason is not (usually) sexism but because he is looking for reassurance that he would not have to crank up the whole stressful and expensive business of interviewing again in the near future.

Questions to Ask the Interviewer

Towards the end of the interview you will generally be asked what question you want to put and in the eyes of many interviewers, the quality of these questions is as important as that of your earlier replies. They demonstrate firstly that you have done your homework on the employer's organisation, secondly that you have thought analytically about their problems and thirdly that you have got some grasp of organising information and seeing the important gaps in it. Again, it is difficult to anticipate what questions you might ask but here are some that you might consider raising:

- Where does the job fit into the organisational structure?
- Why has the job not been filled internally?
- Is it a new position? If not, what happened to the last incumbent and how long did he hold it?
- What do you consider the most important problems to be tackled?
- What do you consider the most important objectives in terms of markets, products or administrative goals?
- What resources would be made available to reach them? What significant constraints are there?
- How is success measured?

None of these questions, it should be noted, touches the question of salary and conditions and the universal advice given by the experts is that you should not raise these matters, however passionate your interest in them will naturally be, until the interviewer initiates them. Indeed, some career consultants go so far as to say that you should evade the salary issue altogether, refusing even to answer questions about your present or last salary until you have been offered a job. This seems to be questionable advice because, as one recruiter said: 'If a person is going to be awkward in an interview, heaven knows what they will be like in the job.' However, the recommendation *not* to start talking salaries until you are offered the job is soundly based for the simple reason that once they offer you the job you are in a much better position than when they still have several people to choose from. In the meantime you should be turning over in your mind, having now got to the heart of the organisation, whether it beats in tune to yours; which is one of the subjects of the next chapter.

12. Evaluating and Negotiating a Job Offer

Bernard Shaw, as far as is known, had little experience of applying for jobs but, like all good writers, had empathy as the following passage from *Major Barbara* shows:

Undershaft: But Mr. Cusins, this is a serious matter. You are not bringing any capital into the concern.

Cusins: What! No capital! Is my mastery of Greek no capital! Is my access to subtlest thought, the loftiest poetry yet attained by humanity, no capital? My character! My intellect! My life! My career! What Barbara calls my soul! Are these no capital? Say another word and I double my salary.

Undershaft: Be reasonable –

Cusins: Mr. Undershaft, you have my terms. Take them or leave them.

Undershaft: [recovering himself]: Very well, I note your terms, and I offer half.

Cusins: Half!

Undershaft: Half.

Cusins: You call yourself a gentleman; and you offer me half!

Undershaft: I do not call myself a gentleman; but I offer you half.

Salary negotiations are not usually quite as idiosyncratic as this, but there are some that run it close. Professor Cusins was applying for a job in Mr. Undershaft's arms factory and there certainly are those among the ranks of

young graduates who have as misplaced an idea of the
relevance of their academic qualifications as he did, but
without being in Professor Cusins's privileged position.
He happened also to be Undershaft's prospective son-in-
law. Andrew Undershaft was a highly intelligent, self-
made millionaire and there are certainly entrepreneurs of
that stamp, whose idea of negotiating is not that far
removed from that which Shaw describes. In actual fact
Professor Cusins and Mr. Undershaft were more closely
matched as protagonists than this passage, taken out of
context, indicates. Nevertheless it shows – if in carica-
ture – how you can weaken your negotiating position by
setting your price before you have clearly demonstrated
your ability.

It also encapsulates some other lessons about evaluating, and negotiating with, an employer. In the chapter on
the unadvertised job market, we showed how you can
learn a great deal about an organisation which you have
targeted as a prospective employer by reading about it
and talking to people who know it. But there are many
things that only emerge clearly when you go there
yourself, in the same way as visiting another country,
even for a day, conveys its atmosphere and consequently
something of what life is like there, in a way no indirect
report could. This aspect of the interview – picking up the
general flavour of the organisation and matching it to
your own style and personality in the way discussed in
Chapter 3 – is very important. Anyone who thinks otherwise should re-read the section on headhunters in Chapter 10. These hard-headed professionals, who make a
living by finding highly-priced executives for highly-paid
jobs, spend a great deal of their expensive time getting
the 'feel' of the client organisation before beginning the
search on their behalf.

The One-Man Band

What would they have made of Andrew Undershaft? If
you read the play he comes over as a man who steers by
the seat of his pants, makes decisions on impulse, has
some rather eccentric ideas about economics but is also
shrewd and not unkind. Apart from that he is a total
autocrat whose partner Lazarus is treated as a diligent
cipher. Such men are by no means uncommon in British
industry and working for them or their organisation has

clear implications for the job seeker. Professor Hunt, who also stresses the importance in interviews of 'trying to figure out the organisational climate' says:

> A very dominant chief executive like X (he mentioned an international publishing tycoon) tends to attract people in his own image – he hires himself over and over again and his beliefs and philosophies dominate.

This theme was also developed in a private paper circulated by the headhunters, Eurosurvey. It compared the task of an executive arriving in such a company to that of a parachutist landing on a terrain which 'looks flat and bare with few apparently significant features and one landowner'. It went on to say:

> The flat and bare estate reflects a company managed by a single man, generally its founder. He holds all the power because he makes practically all the decisions . . . The owner-manager who appoints a deputy does so rather as though he personally were giving birth to an heir.

In such an organisation, the closer you are to the top, the larger the shadow of the chief executive looms, but his personal style is also apt to be reflected lower down the ladder, not only in matters of policy but in the kind of people that are appointed – and of those who leave. A rather unpleasant bullying chief executive often pays good money but will cause the flight of all but yes-men and the toughest and most tenacious careerists; which is why asking about the rate of staff turnover is a good question to raise at the interview. This is a more significant indicator than newspaper stories about a particular company which may denigrate or glamourise a situation in the interests of good copy. Chief executives, as one recruiter said, are seldom either the ogres or geniuses that journalists represent them as being.

Family Companies

Another kind of parachute descent identified by Eurosurvey is into:

> Hilly wooded land with little villages (which) describe the family company where generations of sons, nephews and

171

cousins have each dug entrenchments and built their own little fortresses.

In such companies, as well as those run by authoritarian individuals, there are often informal hierarchies that are far more important than those that exist on paper.

Speaking for a moment from personal experience, in my first job I went overseas to work for a subsidiary of a British company. My post was rather undefined – I was a kind of general assistant to the manager, an autocrat of great energy and ability. He had a secretary, whom I shall call Nancy, and in my first weeks there I gave a party for a few people in the office. I did not invite Nancy, a married lady a good few years older than I was – not because I had any particular feelings about her one way or the other –but because I saw no real reason why I should invite a secretary who was not even working for me. What I did not realise was that Nancy expected to be invited to such occasions – it was a small office where people mixed socially a good deal – and was mortally offended that I had not asked her. Further- more, she and my boss were close personal friends. She thought – and made it clear to my boss that she thought – that I was taking an unduly lofty view of what was in fact a humble role as an executive 'gofer' (a lovely American term for someone who is asked to 'go for' tea, coffee, the boss's cigarettes, or whatever). My subsequent career never really recovered from offending Nancy. I had not grasped the real power structure of that office.

Some years later – in my next job, in fact – I went to work for the British subsidiary of an American company. My colleague was a charming, clever and amusing man whose interest in the company's business was minimal. He was, however, the son of the chairman and though he had no place at all in the theoretical power structure of that company, he and his father got on extremely well. He and I also got on well and since this was a known fact back in New York, I was treated by senior executives there with a respect quite unrelated to my status as manager of a not particu- larly important subsidiary. It was not due to any calculation on my part, but I had accidentally put my foot on the correct rung in that particular corporate ladder.

Where such arbitrary hierarchy relationships exist under the surface – or where it emerges in the interview that this is a problem you may have to contend with – it is very important to establish what the limits of your real power would be. They may be quite different from those which are employed in the job title or even the job description.

Another important matter to sort out is where the ladder of advancement is. It is less common now than it used to be for family companies to be completely dominated by members of the family, though it is highly likely that they will have their feet in advantageous positions on the rungs of the ladder. The question to be sorted out here is one of degree. How many outsiders are there in the kind of senior positions you might ultimately have your eye on? If members of the family are clustered on the organisation tree like starlings at migration time, it is obviously not a good long-term prospect for the ambitious and may even be a frustrating experience in the short term unless ability is as thick as blood.

Public Companies

This problem does not usually occur in public companies but although they are often represented as bland 'faceless corporations' – the civil service, as it were, of the capitalist system – they, too, have idiosyncracies which the job seeker should try to establish before and during the interview. Anthony Jay's interesting book *Corporation Man*, which has been referred to several times, is in fact an attempt to establish a kind of anthropology of the organisation, based on the fact that companies, like countries, have a culture of their own:

> When we say 'What is Ford like to work for?', 'What is IBM like to deal with?', 'That's typical of Dupont', we are assuming a continuing identity going right through the corporation and going back over many years. Insofar as we can generalise about nations – 'Just like the Italians', 'Typically German' – it is this same cultural tradition, not a specifically Italian or German combination of genes, that we are referring to.

Jay believes that a number of factors make up the character of an organisation and these are subject to change or pressure once the organisation ceases to be successful. In a magazine, for instance, it is often the case that either the editorial or the advertising side will dominate the contents and that dominance will only be challenged by outside events.

The question of what part of the organisation is currently making the running is also an important one from the point of view of determining where the ladders of advancement are. Although large organisations tend to have more clearly established hierarchies than smaller ones, the status of particular functions varies – quite often in relation to the background of the chief executive. Speaking of who dominates the internal status system, Jay says:

> In the one firm it will be the scientist, in another the salesman. In a healthy firm the status ranking will follow the priority order of importance of the firm's success and survival. The convulsion comes when the conditions of survival change faster than the normal organic change of the individuals on the status ladder.

This last point is an important one for younger job seekers to consider in making their career choice in a time of rapid technological change. Jay quotes the example of the engineering industry which was dominated by production people in the 50s and 60s whereas the actual skills needed for survival were in marketing – as the case of the British motorcycle industry showed. The question to try to establish in your research and at the interview is whether the company is run by people who are adaptable and responsive to change or by those who hope, more or less secretly, that it won't happen.

Salary Negotiations

The characteristics of these various organisations also give some clue as to how to conduct salary negotiations. This is becoming an increasingly important skill to develop not only in the unadvertised job market where, in the nature of things the salary is an unknown quantity, but even in the advertised sector. As we have stated earlier, the custom is creeping in from the USA for salaries not to be given in advertisements. This is probably most often true of smaller or family firms or in individualistically run companies like Mr. Undershaft's. Clearly Mr. Undershaft had no salary structure and in the play he was, in fact, prepared to pay the novice Professor Cusins more than he was probably worth. This might not happen in real life but there certainly *are* firms whose idea of salary structures bears no relation to the orderly methods recommended in Michael Armstrong's textbook *Handbook of Personnel Management and Practice*. He suggests that salaries should be based either on the position of the job in the hierarchy, the skill involved in it or length of service – in some cases elements of all three. There are, however, a great many smaller firms where the criteria tend to be based at one end of the scale on how little they can get away with and at the other how much they need to pay to attract the right person without offending long term employees who have been doing jobs of similar status for less money.

From the point of view of job seekers, the advantage of such situations is that they give wider scope for negotiating. Professor Cusins, in the end, secured three-fifths of his figure. The fact that he then had to ask someone whether three-fifths was more or less than one half would not exactly have heightened his standing with his future colleagues. As Mr. Undershaft's heir-presumptive this may not have mattered unduly, but for lesser mortals you really have to demonstrate your ability very clearly to those around you if you come into a firm on a much higher salary than they are getting. It is also likely that even if you are the winner now, the absence of an established structure will mean that you will eventually be the loser unless you are prepared to fight for every rise.

The problem, on the other hand, is that if you come in at too low a figure, you never catch up because every increase starts from that base. This naturally raises the question whether you should price yourself low in order to get a particular job. Expert advice is that you should not go below market rates. A sensible employer would take the view that you can either do the job or you cannot. If you cannot, you are not worth having at all. If you can, you are worth the rate for the job. Thus a drop in salary should only be acceptable in the context of moving to a smaller company, to a job with less responsibility, to making a change of direction in career terms or going to an area where salary rates are lower because the cost of living is lower. In these circumstances, taking a drop from your last salary will be credible, especially if you have other income to make up the loss – maybe from a pension or a well-invested golden handshake.

This does not mean that an employer will not try and get

you at his lowest figure. Quite often, for instance, a salary *range* is stated in an advertisement. The advice given by consultants is always to go for the higher amount but not even to begin to think about negotiating until you get towards the end of the interview and have had a chance to demonstrate your value. If the issue is raised by the interviewer before then (assuming no definite figure is advertised), the best course of action is to stall politely by saying that you would like to know more about the job before talking salaries.

The familiar ploy, when the interviewer has no salary structure but would like to find out what he or she can get for you, is to ask what you are currently earning. This will indicate that they have no idea how much to pay, at least within very broad limits, and it is possible, if you play your cards right, to get very much more than you were earning before – but *not* if you say how much that was. It would, of course, be discourteous to refuse to answer the question but you can say that it was a complicated package of salary and other benefits that makes comparison of salary difficult; or you can give a figure but state – with evidence, of course (this is another question you should prepare for) – that the two jobs are so different that you would not regard the one salary as being the basis for discussing the other, except in very broad terms.

It is, in fact, true that fringe benefits can make salary comparisons very difficult. The danger is that one tends to take them for granted in an existing salary and not to take account of the fact that they enhance its real value very considerably. A company car, for instance, is reckoned to be worth at least £3,000 a year and at more senior levels there is often a wide range of perks beyond that. (It has, in fact, been suggested by cynical observers that in highly taxed Western countries fringe benefits occupy a somewhat similar place to the much censured 'backhander' in developing economies.) Thus a high salary with few perks may, in fact, be worth a lot less in real terms than a lower salary with a generous range of fringe benefits. It is the total remuneration package of one job against another that should be compared, though negotiation should begin with salary rather than benefits.

To what extent the one can, with advantage, be traded off against the other depends to some extent on your age. The older executive, sacrificing a high level of salary for a mess of perks should be aware of the fact that pension will be based on salary only and, as we stated earlier, if you start from too low a level, it is very difficult to catch up.

Some candidates, of course, are in a stronger negotiation position than others. Clearly, if you have a job with which you are reasonably satisfied, you are much better placed, even in psychological terms, than someone who is not so fortunate. The same thing is true of the person who is already considering more than one offer. Career consultants claim that on the principle that it never rains but it pours, this is not an uncommon situation. After months of searching, it suddenly all happens. In that case, tell the interviewer when he or she makes the offer and ask for a couple of days to think it over. If the only doubt in your mind is one of remuneration, you might at this point use the other offer as a lever – but only if it is genuine or if you are supremely confident of your ability to bluff without ever being found out.

The Letter of Acknowledgement

In the normal course of events, the employer will confirm their offer in writing but it does no harm, if an offer has been made at the end of a job interview, to sum up what you remember was discussed in the way of terms, signify your acceptance of them and thus initiate a confirmatory letter. Indeed, even if the interview is unsuccessful, a thank-you note is never wasted. Who knows? Sometimes the first choice gets an even better offer from another source and you are in line for the runners-up prize.

Part Two

ALTERNATIVES

13. Temporary Jobs and Job Sharing

There are two schools of thought about taking on temporary jobs if you are out of work. One is that you should let nothing distract you from the job search. Indeed, it must be said that the task of tracking down unadvertised vacancies through reading, research and contact interviews is extremely time consuming and doesn't leave much time for other things. The other is that taking on temporary assignments, provided they are roughly at your level, is a point in your favour when it comes to an interview for the job you really want. It keeps you in touch with the world of work, it may even expand your experience and it shows an ability to fight back. The debate may, of course, be settled for you by sheer financial necessity. Unemployment benefit falls into the category of being too much to die on but not really quite enough to live off – especially as you get older – and if, for whatever reason, you have not been able to get more than the statutory redundancy settlement, you may have no option but to try to get some sort of temporary post.

The trouble with such jobs is that at more senior levels they are quite hard to come by. They also occur in such a random way that an organised search on your own is unlikely to be fruitful. They are seldom advertised, though *Executive Post* does include a weekly list of temporary jobs with a duration of between three months and a year, mostly at fairly modest salary levels of £90-150 a week and mostly in local government.

The reason why good temporary vacancies are hard to come by is that they are *ad hoc* events. They cannot be planned for, either by the job seeker or the employer. If you walk through the door at the right time the job is yours. A day too soon and the emergency has not yet happened. A week too late and they have found some other way of coping with it.

That, at least, has been the traditional way of looking at temporary employment, but it may be changing. Economic uncertainty makes firms reluctant to commit themselves to taking on people permanently. Someone may have left unexpectedly, but are they sure they really want a long-term replacement? A rush job may need to be completed against a deadline, but what happens when it is over? A business opportunity may need expert investigation, but who has the time to undertake it and if someone is hired for this purpose, who knows beforehand whether it will be worth pursuing? In such situations it would be folly to take on permanent staff. One answer is to sub-contract such an assignment to self-employed freelances or to a small business outside. Another is to go to an agency specialising in temporary employment and bring in someone for a short period who can take care of the problem. Thus, if the demand keeps up, or the person concerned turns out to be a success, they can be offered permanent employment. In the chapter on interviewing we pointed out what an imperfect selection tool the interview was by itself. Actually working with someone for a few weeks or months has to be an infinitely better way of evaluating their potential contribution than an hour or two's interview, no matter how skilfully conducted. And though permanent appointments generally have a trial period built into them, they are rather like trial marriages; the implied commitment is a strong one and not at all easy to break without a lot of ill-feeling.

There are some signs, though they are not as yet substantial, that there is an increasing awareness by employers of the advantages of taking on people temporarily and not just in the traditional areas of junior jobs during holiday periods. Manpower, a world-wide job agency specialising in supplying temporary staff have some 90 offices in the UK and have lately made considerable efforts to trade up to middle managerial level and even beyond, apparently with a good deal of success. They impose no limitations on age and there is no limit, either, on the length of assignments they handle – the minimum is a day and Manpower's London office say they have someone on their books who has been working on the same temporary assignment for fourteen years! It would be more usual, in those circumstances, for the person concerned to be taken on permanently and this is, apparently, quite a common event. No extra charge is made to the employer in that case – it is, incidentally he who pays Manpower's charges, not the temporary employee for whom work is found.

People applying to be put on Manpower's books are given an interview, an aptitude test and are asked to fill in quite a detailed application form. Manpower try to match people to jobs – that is, they will try to place them as closely as possible to the level at which they were previously employed. They also try to maintain parity of job rates with existing permanent staff working at the same level.

Manpower's clients are drawn from the public as well as the private sectors – they include the Coal Board, British Gas and most of the top 1,000 companies in the UK, though significantly, Denis Bruce, the manager of their London operation sees their growth as coming mainly in the less conservative companies. For this reason they are also progressive in their attitudes towards who they take on. For instance, they take a liberal stance on race – by no means universal in the job market – and will take on young graduates and school leavers without work experience provided they have good academic qualifications. As far as managerial jobs are concerned, Bruce says:

> We have a wide range of assignments at the top end of the market and we feel pretty confident that we can find a job for someone at middle management level within a couple of weeks of putting them on our books.

Manpower, however, are relative newcomers to the concept of temporary assignments at more senior levels. Apart from a few professional bodies or associations like the Institute of Directors who maintain a register of members available for temporary work, there are still only a few commercial agencies operating at management levels, though a firm called Intex has been involved in it for the past few years. They have about 1,000 temporary job seekers on their books at any one time, ranging from the mid-thirties to retired people and they reckon that 10–15 per cent of them will get an assignment in the course of a year, with an average duration of 2-3 months. They have made some impressive placements, a number of which have turned into permanent appointments, but one gets the impression that the demand from senior level job seekers for such assignments is greater than the supply of them. Significantly neither they, nor another firm specialising in this field, Executive Standby, advertise for fear that they would be swamped by enquiries – not from companies whom they mail discreetly with names on their register, but from individual executives who want to go on it.

The problem is that at this level their objectives are too similar to those of orthodox management consultants, though they claim, probably with some justification, that consultants cannot put their hands to anything like the range of specialised expertise that is available in the pool of unemployed executives. Management consultants, moreover, are much more expensive than the associate executives (as Intex terms them) who are leased out at rates of between £75 and £200 per day. Particularly for longer term assignments, where rates are to some extent negotiable, a temporary executive works out much cheaper than the services of a fully fledged consultant. Don Lueck, the American managing direction of Intex – it is an international firm and many of their assignments are in fact abroad – believes that their approach is 'a tremendously effective way of creating a market for talent that is now under-used'. He is right, but the trouble is that it needs a lot of publicity and advertising to put the idea over. It is one whose day is likely to come, but perhaps more slowly than it deserves to.[1]

Job Sharing

Another idea which falls into the category of being ahead of its time, in terms of wider acceptance than it ought to have, is job sharing. In this case, though, it is one that has received a good deal of official encouragement. In fact from January 1983 a grant is being paid by the government to employers who introduce it.

Job sharing is not new. Some organisations, most notably the clearing banks and a few public sector employers have been using it for some time, though probably more in order to keep certain employees who would otherwise have had to leave for family reasons than in order to preserve jobs.

The basic principle is simple. It is not part-time work, with which it is sometimes confused, but means that a full-time job is split between two people. There are no hard and fast rules about how this is to be done. In most cases arrangements have been made to work alternate weeks or to split the week in some way. The only real proviso is that salaries, holidays and other benefits are divided pro rata and of course the job itself should be split in such a way that it can be carried out satisfactorily. For instance, it may require job sharers to overlap for the one to pick up progress from the other.

Where this presents no problems – and there obviously are jobs which depend on the consistent touch of one individual – job sharing has a lot to recommend it both from the employer's and the employee's point of view. It has been found, for instance, that the quality of work produced by sharers is higher, simply because at any one time they are less tired than an individual working on their own. In the case of highly skilled jobs the complementary talents of two sharers can also be an asset. At Lancaster University, for instance, there is a lecturing job shared between a husband and wife whose combined expertise is greater than most individuals would be able to bring to the post. One of the features of job sharing seems in fact to be that it is most practicable at the level of professional jobs (doctors, lawyers, teachers) and, on the other end of the scale, in the case of jobs that combine tedium with the need for concentration. What is shift work, after all, other than a form of job sharing?

The problem from the point of view of the job seeker obviously is that no one, other than family or close friends, are going to move over to share their job (and income) with you. But it could happen that employers, tempted by financial help from the government, may start to offer some jobs on a split basis. If this does occur, it seems likely that they will look for ready-made pairs of sharers, rather than yoke unfamiliar partners together. Another possibility is that they will allow two people to share a job rather than make one of them redundant. That indeed is one of the circumstances in which the grant is payable, the other being when job sharing results in an unemployed person being brought back into employment. Ultimately though, the acceptance of job sharing will depend on the result once it is tried on a wider scale, rather than on the fairly modest £750 per job incentive offered to employers by the government scheme.

[1] A most interesting new initiative was announced by the Manpower Services Commission almost on the very day this chapter was written. As a result of the success of a programme pioneered at Durham Business School in an MSC sponsored course under which redundant large company executives were placed temporarily, after an intensive training course, with smaller businesses, it has been decided to extend this programme to several other parts of the country. In the case of Durham's 'Management Extension Programme' it was found that 50 per cent of executives so placed were taken on permanently by the firms taking part in the experiment and a further 25 per cent either found further temporary work or set up in self-employment.

14. Working Abroad

In happier, or at any rate simpler times than these we now
live in, there was an answer to unemployment summed up
in words which will guarantee Mr. Norman Tebbit's im-
mortality: people got on their bikes. This does not mean
that they found jobs where there were none to be had, but
that they went to places where they could be found. They
moved from the country to the cities, from one part of the
country to another, or they emigrated altogether. The 'poor
and huddled masses' who went to America – and indeed to
many other underpopulated or underdeveloped parts of the
world until well into the twentieth century – were to a
large extent Europe's unemployed.

In some ways the process is still going on. In the USA
there has been a good deal of internal migration with
people moving south from the troubled cities and clapped
out industries of the north; and as late as the 1970s a very
considerable number of Britons, many of whom had been
caught by the effect of the oil price rise on European
economies, found jobs in the OPEC states.

The recession of the early eighties has proved rather
more indivisible in global as well as national terms. Even
the OPEC members are not as rich as they used to be
because world economic problems have also affected the
demand for oil. However everything is relative because,
compared to most western countries, they remain very
affluent. In absolute terms it is also true that Britain, with
an unemployment rate of 15 per cent in the normally
prosperous south-east, going beyond 20 per cent in many
parts of the country, is in a worse state than most other
industrial nations. Is this a case for looking at job prospects
abroad?

Up to a point, Lord Copper: to quote Evelyn Waugh's
famously toadying journalist whose answer to career problems was never to disagree with his boss. The problem is

that countries with unemployment rates of a 'mere' 8–10 per cent are not very anxious to do their own nationals out of jobs by allowing in workers from other countries. The last two or three years have seen a great deal of tightening up in the free movement of labour in most industrial countries, and at all levels. For instance Australia, a country which has not only welcomed immigrants for a long time but which is justifiably high up on many people's preferences, now has an unemployment rate which has risen rapidly to over 10 per cent. In consequence, the number of migrants being allowed in has been reduced considerably and new criteria have been introduced for their admission. Family connections are out and what has replaced them is the ability to make a contribution to the Australian economy, either in terms of offering scarce technological skills, or a readiness to move to a less popular part of the country (most of the population live in and around the five major cities) or the ability to create employment by having the resources and qualifications to set up a business in Australia.

The 'Old' Commonwealth Countries and the USA

To some degree limitations of this kind have been set up in all the English-speaking countries that used to accept emigrants from Europe – many of them giving preference to people from Britain. New Zealand, facing unemployment problems for the first time in its history, issues a list of occupations (through its diplomatic offices) from which emigrants will be considered. Permits to work in the USA or Canada are virtually unobtainable except in high technology or energy conservation-related jobs and even South Africa which, until lately has taken all the (white) immigrants it could lay its hands on, is reported to be clamping down.

There *are* jobs to be had in all of those countries, but what you cannot now do is what people used to do when they had no particular job to go to: which was to get a temporary work or residential permit and then gradually drift into permanent status if they liked it there. The only way you can be sure of being allowed to work in most of these countries now is either if a British or other foreign employer sends you to work in a branch located there or if a local employer recruits you here and gets a work permit for you. Both of these things do happen, though in the nature of things such jobs tend to be found more through the advertised than the unadvertised sector. Apart from national newspapers where the jobs shown are at the top end of the market, overseas vacancies are to be found in the specialist and trade press. They also crop up in *Executive Post*.

Europe
What about Europe, though, and specifically the EEC? At the end of 1981 there were reportedly something like 250,000 British people working in various EEC countries, with Germany at the top of the list, followed by Holland, France and Italy. Quite a number of them were technicians and construction workers because the 'harmonisation' of professional jobs, giving professionals the right to move freely from one part of the EEC to another without having to take up local qualifications, has been very slow. Even if this were not the case, though, there would still be the language barrier. Most younger people in the EEC speak English with a fluency that puts our general standard of ability to speak their language to shame, but for everyday commercial or professional purposes you cannot get by without being able to speak the language of the country in which you are working. It is only at the very highest levels of scientific and technical skill that you can survive professionally otherwise, and then only provided you are dealing mainly with your peers, because in those circles English has established itself as the *lingua franca*. Curiously enough, manual workers also seem to survive without much initial command of the language of the host country – perhaps because Europeans have become used to the 'guest worker' concept.

Employment conditions in Europe, as elsewhere, have worsened since 1981 and the guest workers have proved embarrassingly difficult to get rid of. Impossibly so, in fact, if they came from within the EEC because in theory, at least, they cannot be made to go home. On the contrary; under Community law, if you have registered as unemployed for more than a month in one member country (including the UK, of course), you can go job seeking for up to three months in any EEC country of your choice, while still drawing benefit from the country where you started out. If you do succeed in getting a job but lose it after a month, then the level of unemployment benefit of that, and not your own country, is paid to you as long as you stay.

In most EEC countries benefit, if you lose your job, is much more generous than in the UK – 70 per cent of last salary for the first nine months of unemployment in Germany, 80 per cent for the first six months in Holland, 70 per cent for the first three months in France. The snag of trying your luck in the EEC is that you would be unlikely to get a job in present economic conditions without a good command of the language of the country concerned. At the same time UK benefit rates would not give you enough funds to sustain a search in another country unless you can stay with friends. It is also reported that if you do get a job and lose it, pressure is put on you to leave by creating difficulties over renewal of the residence permit which is still needed by citizens of EEC countries if they come from abroad. The French are apparently particularly expert at this form of harassment.

OPEC

Unemployment is not a problem in these countries or at any rate not yet and not at the level at which people are mainly recruited from abroad: professional, managerial and exeuctive. Nevertheless you still need a permit to work in them which a local employer or a locally based foreign company will have no difficulty in getting, provided they can demonstrate the job needs to be done.

The ones that fall into this category cover quite a wide range. In the African and Arab OPEC nations there is still enormous scope for technical skills in virtually every field and at every level from senior managers down to skilled supervisors and tradesmen. There is also quite a demand for instructors which may, in the long term, augur ill for expatriates because what these countries are obviously and naturally trying to do is to replace expatriates with their own people. At the same time there is a slowly growing trend to move away from purely technical jobs into what the jargon calls 'infrastructural' ones: the mangerial and service areas that develop as economies grow around them. It is here, as we have pointed out in earlier chapters, that there are sometimes interesting opportunities for older executives and enquiries for their services may be directed to the UK through professional institutes as well as through contacts in the unadvertised job field.

The Far East

Scope in the Far East is more limited, except in Brunei – a small but oil-rich country with very close links to the UK. In Hongkong, Malaysia and Singapore, vacancies normally occur only at more senior management levels or their equivalent in professional areas. Here there is still quite a demand for European-trained businessmen and lawyers because of the importance of overseas trade connections and first-hand knowledge of procedures and personalities. There is little scope, though, in the more junior ranks because of the presence of the formidably intelligent, immensely hardworking and much cheaper to employ indigenous population, much of it Chinese.

Developing Countries

There are some 160 countries which are designated as 'developing' and expatriates are employed in most of those which were formerly British possessions. To a large extent they are in public sector jobs, mostly in the technical, agricultural, teaching or other professional spheres. They are employed either by the UK government under its technical co-operation scheme or by overseas government receiving some kind of aid from the Overseas Development Administration which enables it to hire skilled expatriates whom they could not otherwise afford. Salaries are based on UK levels for the job in question, plus some additional allowance. There is an important difference between working directly for a British government agency and working in an overseas post which is only subsidised from the UK: in the first instance you have to pay UK tax, in the second you are taxed at local rates which may be a good deal lower.

For those to whom a job and the experience of living abroad is more important than money there are also opportunities for voluntary work in developing countries. The largest agency in this sphere is VSO (Voluntary Service Overseas) which places about 500 people a year in a very wide variety of trades and skills, ranging from butchers and bakers to teachers, accountants and engineers. They are quite prepared to take unemployed people, though not usually those without work experience, and recruit mainly in the early spring and autumn. Unlike the jobs described in the preceding paragraph VSO posts are seldom advertised and if you are interested in this type of work, the best plan is to apply to VSO for an interview. They take people between 20 and 65, though the average age of VSO workers seems to be in the late twenties. If you are generally suitable and have a skill they are interested in you will be placed on their register.

The pay, of course, is very modest. It is related to local rates for the job, although you will be given an equipment grant and a small bonus at the end of the employment period which has to be not less than two years.

More suitable, perhaps, for older people thinking of working abroad on this basis is BESO (British Executive Services Overseas). They operate in conjunction with the Institute of Directors and, from a register of about 1,000 people, offer about 130 assignments a year at senior professional, executive and managerial levels. On average, these jobs last about six months and they are unpaid except for a very small allowance, though food and suitable accommodation are provided. The advantage of the BESO scheme, apart from the fact that it involves a shorter commitment in terms of time than VSO, is that apparently it quite often leads to offers of paid jobs or consultancies in the countries concerned. Both VSO and BESO have women as well as men on their register.

Working Conditions Abroad

Working abroad has a great deal to recommend it provided you go into it with your eyes open. The trouble is that a fair number of people are so dazzled by the thought of salaries which, as well as being usually much higher than in the UK – and tax free as well, in many OPEC states – accompanied by generous fringe benefits, that they do not stop to think of the drawbacks. One of these is climate – spending months on end in hot humid places, often with a very limited amount of company, is by no means the same as three weeks on the Costa Packet. The other is culture shock. Though there are large expatriate communities in the main centres, you still have to get used to very different living conditions if you go to strict Moslem countries like Saudi Arabia or Libya. These conditions often weigh more heavily on wives, unless they can get jobs as well, because the men at least have their work to keep them occupied. In most Middle East countries, incidentally, it is difficult for single women to get jobs and often life is not pleasant for them there, even if they do; for instance, women are not allowed to drive unaccompanied in Saudi Arabia.

If you are thinking of working abroad the best plan is to begin by studying current salary rates and fringe benefits on offer in the countries and jobs in which you are interested. The latter are particularly important because unless accommodation, holiday travel, children's education and medical attention are paid for or heavily subsidised, they can tear huge holes out of the most imposing salary figures. In the case of European firms, remuneration packages are by now pretty standard, but some local firms as well as those less experienced in the conditions in question offer variances that may be less in your favour in some crucial respects. The time to negotiate is before you accept the job, not when you find your 'free' accommodation has neither furniture nor telephone.

15. Self-Employment

One of the few growth industries over the last two or three years has been telling people how to run their own business. The Small Firms Centre offices which are dotted round the country – you can get the address of your nearest one by dialling 100 and asking for Freefone 2444 – are backed up in rural areas by CoSIRA (Council for Small Industries in Rural Areas). Then there is the Scottish Development Agency's Small Business Division and the Welsh Development Agency's Small Business Division and the Local Enterprise Development Unit in Northern Ireland. Below them there is a growing network of local enterprise initiatives whose activities range from advising on management buy-outs where groups of employees bind together to acquire the assets of insolvent employers, to telling individuals how to get finance, how to present their case to a bank, how to get planning permission or even where to get suitable premises.[1] They also send people on small business courses which range at the upper end of the scale to 16-week programmes at one of four business schools (Manchester, Durham, London or Glasgow) to much shorter courses given by various technical colleges and polytechnics; there is, for instance, a weekend course given by the UrBED Enterprise Development Unit in London which is linked to the City University Business School. Usually, if you are over 19 and have been away from full-time education for two years or more, you will be eligible for a TOPS grant, in which case the course is free and you will also receive an attendance allowance for going on it – the amounts are detailed on leaflet TSD 103 which is available at jobcentres. If you want further information you should ask to see the employment adviser dealing with TOPS (Training Opportunity Schemes) there. You will, however, have to take a test to assess your suitability for the course you have in mind.

The existence of help for those thinking of self-employment, whatever form such help takes, is to be welcomed because ultimately the sad fact must be faced that there are quite a lot of people whose chances of finding another job as an employee are slim, no matter with what energy and ingenuity they apply the lessons in this book to the job search. Another sad fact that must be faced is that the failure rates among new businesses are very high – about 70 per cent, it is thought. Furthermore, and contrary to the belief that by forming a limited company you can go bust with other people's money, these failures are nearly always costly to the owners of the businesses concerned. How can you avoid sharing their fate?

Significantly, most of the courses and books on the subject place a good deal of emphasis on self-assessment, the importance of which, in the orthodox job search, has already been pointed out in Chapter 5: *Unpeeling the Labels*. If you take an honest and dispassionate look at some of the personal characteristics listed in that chapter and you rate badly in areas that are important for people running their own business (self-discipline, practicality, determination, judgment etc.) you are likely to find self-employment a thorny path.

Furthermore, these are only the starting points. Dr. Ronnie Lessem, the director of UrBED and a man who has had much experience in training budding entrepreneurs, has identified further characteristics that distinguish them from persons who function better within an organisation. For instance, he feels that entrepreneurs work by intuition rather than logic, think of opportunities rather than problems, operate through informal contacts rather than official channels, see business as a series of dramas rather than a set of routines. This may sound a trifle abstract, but it provides a framework for the fact that moving from an organisation to self-employment is a considerable culture shock. People launching out on their own after years of working for others tend to forget what a warm comfortable place the organisation is. 'Someone' looks after the PAYE and VAT returns, 'someone' prepares the accounts, sends out goods, serves the customers, makes out invoices, orders the stationery, types letters and makes the coffee. If you count all the activities undertaken by 'someone' in your present or last job, it adds up to a formidable list of things you will have to do for yourself as a self-employed person.

You can, of course, arrange to have some of them done for you – at a price. But in the early stages of your business that could mean a serious drain on your slender income and the fact still remains that when you get important functions done outside, it diminishes the amount of control you can exercise. In a small organisation it is the owner who carries the can for anything that goes wrong.

In a big organisation it is, as we all know, a common ploy to blame the accounts department, or the warehouse of whatever. That is something you can no longer do if you run your own business and one of the hardest lessons for the self-employed is that whereas, as an employee, one might feel resentful about being a cog in a wheel, being the wheel yourself is no picnic.

Working With Others

One obvious alternative is to go into business with other people. Certainly this helps with one of the problems of self-employment: the loneliness of working on your own. The office or factory is a very sociable place and in our fragmented and private world, contact, gossip or even formal meetings at work seem to become at least as important as the job itself. But if you go into business with a partner, you ought to be sure that he or she is someone who can make a contribution to the venture and not merely link yourself to someone who is fun to have around. Some very successful partnerships are made up of people who have very little in common outside working hours, though the mutual trust of friendship is certainly an additional asset.

What is meant by 'contribution' is not so much 'money' but that they have complementary skills and qualities to contribute; one, for instance, may be wonderfully efficient at administration and another equally good at selling. People working together in this way may set up a formal partnership or they may turn themselves into directors of a limited company – which course you choose depends on the nature of the activity and it is a matter on which it is important to get legal and financial advice.

Another advantage of working with other people is that it can lighten the workload. Most self-employed people comment that it is far harder work than they ever expected. 'Yes, it means freedom,' said one new entrepreneur taking the London Business School course. 'Freedom to work seven days a week, sixteen hours a day.'

Some people do thrive on that sort of thing, though it is hard on their families. Going into business with others at least means that you can get away for an annual holiday and stay at home when you are sick without getting a nervous breakdown to go with physical illness.

Money

Another important distinction between self-employment and working for others is that you are using your own money. This sounds so obvious as to hardly be worth saying, but people starting their own business do not always grasp the implications of the fact that you cannot just indent (to 'someone' again) for office equipment, furniture, tools or even writing materials – you have to pay them yourself and unless the purchase is justified in terms of the income it brings into the business it should not be made. Never buy what you can borrow, beg or hire unless you have a long-term, economically viable use for it.

The temptation to start out in a bigger way than circumstances warrant is heightened by the fact that these days funds are easier to raise than they used to be. Recently there was a story in the *Sunday Times* that illustrated both this point and the perils related to it. It told of a small firm which had been set up by a group of redundant executives to produce kits for self-assembly furniture. It was lent £100,000 by the Manpower Services Commission towards it wage bill, £125,000 from the GLC to refurbish some workshops, £17,500 from the Borough of Lambeth for buying machinery and, on top of all this, a substantial sum from the government's own business funding operation, The Industrial and Commercial Finance Coporation (ICFC). Heading its story, KILLED WITH KINDNESS: Firm That Was Given A Big New Factory When All It Needed Was A Railway Arch, it described a classic case of a firm that went under because it saddled itself with overheads and interest charges that its anticipated scale of business in the foreseeable future could not possibly justify.

Not many enterprises have had misguided fairy godmothers push golden spoons into their mouths with quite such abandon, but it is not at all difficult to get finance for a small business. Usually this is by way of a bank overdraft tied to a personal guarantee or some form of security which over-rides the 'limited liability' of a limited company. The idea of a limited company is that if the worst comes to the worst the liability of its shareholders for its debts are confined to the value of the issued share capital – which need only be a somewhat nominal sum – and to the assets of the company. Their private assets cannot be touched if the firm goes under, but the bank's guarantee, being a personal one, has to be met regardless.

The risks of doing anything too rash are to some extent reduced by the fact that, even so, the bank will not simply hand you the money on request. They will ask you to make out a good case for what would normally be a substantial loan or overdraft and quite a number of them now produce free pamphlets which tell people thinking of approaching the bank for funds to start a business what sort of things the manager would want to know. The key document would be a cash flow forecast. This formidable sounding term means no more than making a detailed, month by month estimate, over about a year, of how much money you will need each month and how much you expect to have coming in. Since it is all too easy to overlook vital outgoings in the course of preparing such a forecast, it is worth getting help from an accountant with it.

Even if you are in the happy position of not having to borrow, this is an invaluable exercise. Where you are planning a service activity it will help you schedule your workload and identify the right mix of jobs to look for. Some months, for instance, it may be more advantageous to take on an assignment that will bring in a quick injection of cash rather than something more profitable that will take longer to pay off. If you are going into manufacturing it will prompt you to look at your costs. Should you be thinking of buying a going business, a cash flow forecast will make you look more closely at the present owner's claims about his revenues, the value of his inventories and possibly to focus more sharply on the reason why he wants to sell. Indeed you should look at your own revenue forecasts as critically as if you were buying a business from a third party. More things go wrong during the 'learning curve' phase at the beginning of a business than most people anticipate. If the circumstances which determine the success of a venture leave no margin for error you should consider changing your plans in some way to take account of the inevitable manifestations of Murphy's Law.

The Viability of the Idea

An alert and experienced bank manager will probably spot the signs of a business plan that depends too much on everything going right. What he cannot tell is whether the concept itself is a sound one: that is, whether there is a demand for whatever it is you are proposing to make or do at a price that will show you some profit and whether you can reach the market economically. These are essential conditions for success and only you can judge them. In retailing you have to offer something that people cannot get at the big name multiples, with all the advantages these have of national advertising, an established reputation and High Street sites: you could, for instance, offer longer opening hours, perhaps, or a more exotic product. In manufacturing you have to produce something for which there is a large enough demand – and also a continuing one – but not so large that bigger, stronger competitors will be tempted to move in on you before you are ready to fight them off. In the service sector – and indeed in all forms of activity where you cannot afford a prominent location – you will have to find ways of making yourself known to customers. It has been said that the world will beat a path to the door of anyone who builds a better mousetrap. True; but only if they know where your door is and only if your method is cost effective compared to other ways of doing the same job, like getting a cat.

[1] A directory of their addresses is given in the bibliography

Select Bibliography

Self-Help Books

The BBC Small Business Guide, Colin Barrow (BBC Publications). Up to date, inexpensive and remarkably comprehensive guide to all sources of information and help for starting and running new or small businesses.

Changing Your Job, G. Golzen and Philip Plumbley (Daily Telegraph/Kogan Page). Has gone through many editions and printings since it first came out in 1971 and though modesty precludes one from saying much about it, it is generally considered to be one of the better 'nuts and bolts' books. Written mainly for executives in mid career.

Coping with Interviews, Martin Higham (New Opportunity Press). Aimed mainly at school leavers and young graduates. The author writes regularly in *Graduate Post* on this subject.

Focus on Redundancy, Fred Kemp et al (Kogan Page). Does not give much advice on job hunting. Contains many genuinely useful addresses and information sources, but the authors seem to be unsure whether the book is for job seekers or firms faced with the problems of making people redundant.

Getting the Job You Want, H. Dowding and S. Boyce (Ward Lock). Useful but expensive for only 96 pages. Really just a collection of check lists with no background on how the market actually operates.

Getting a New Job, Consumers' Association (Hodder & Stoughton). Like all CA publications, sound, sensible, accurate and good on legal aspects. Applicable at all levels, but not terribly inspiring to read.

A Guide to Executive Re-Employment, C. Dudeney (Macdonald & Evans). A useful book, widely used on PER courses. A bit whimsical in places, though.

A Guide to Successful Job-Hunting, PER. Free from PER

offices and a useful, sensible starter which tells how to prepare job applications and write CVs.

Guerilla Tactics in the Job Market, T. Jackson (Bantam). A mass market paperback in the USA. Contains some useful hints, but its prose style is distressing.

How to be Interviewed, D. McKenzie Davey BIM (British Institute of Management). Short but useful refresher worth going through on your way to an interview.

How to Find a New Job, Lorne Smith (Lorne Smith Publications). Self-published by the author and more of an extended pamphlet than a book, but within its limits quite good on legal and statutory aspects.

How to Get a Better Job, C. P. Stephenson (Thorson). Aimed at lower middle management, sales reps etc. and somewhat unsophisticated in its approach, though sensible enough. Much of the advice is on the basic side – e.g. that you should wear a clean shirt at the interview.

How to Get a Job, Marjorie Harris (IPM(Institute of Personnel Management)). Also aimed mainly at the young job seeker. Says nothing very original, but a sound introduction.

How to Survive Unemployment, Robert Nathan and Michael Syrett (IPM). One of the few books so far to give wider coverage to alternatives to regular employment.

Job and Career Building, R. German and P. Arnold (Harper & Row). Another American book which is hard to get in the UK. Good chapters on the unadvertised job market and on conducting a self-marketing campaign.

Moving Up Quickly – How to Use Executive Job Hunting Techniques to Land a Better Job, T. L. Weck (John Wiley). In spite of the unilluminating title, a good sensible American book, easy to read, jargon free and largely applicable to the UK as well as the USA.

Out of the Rut, J. and M. Korving (BBC Publications). An unconventional but helpful workbook of DIY exercises based on case studies of four hypothetical but by no means unbelievable individuals thinking of a career change.

The Survivor's Guide to Unemployment and Redundancy, Joy Melville (Corgi). Does not tell you a great deal about job hunting – more about coping with financial and emotional problems of redundancy.

What Colour is Your Parachute?, R. N. Bolles (Ten Speed Press). A wildly successful American book, hard to get here though it has been in and out of the US bestseller list for years. Contains much sensible advice, though a lot of it is not relevant outside the USA and sophisticated readers might find its bible-belt style somewhat off-putting. Worth having a look at if you are applying to a US company.

Working for Yourself, G. Golzen (Daily Telegraph/Kogan Page). Again modesty precludes but this book, now in its fifth edition, is regarded by impartial people (such as reviewers) as one of the better books on the subject. The same is true of same author's *Working Abroad*, another Daily Telegraph/Kogan Page Publication.

Background Reading

The Collapse of Work, C. Jenkins and B. Sherman (Eyre Methuen). Influential, interesting, if at times wrong-headed book by two prominent trade union leaders.

Corporation Man, Anthony Jay (Cape). Entertaining, if occasionally far-fetched attempt to develop an anthropology of organisation. Some genuine insights make it a good read before you start your next job.

Job Sharing: A Guide for Employees, New ways to work. Good, concise account of what the concept involves. There is a companion book written for employers.

Handbook of Personnel Management and Practice, M. Armstrong (Kogan Page). A widely used textbook which gives some insight into how recruiters operate and how salary structures are determined.

The Headhunters, R. McKinnon (Scope Books). Very interesting journalistic study of what headhunters do and how they view their role in the job market.

Lateral Thinking, E. De Bono (Penguin). De Bono's first (and best) book on how to break out of conventional – in his terms vertical – ways of looking at problems.

Passages, Gail Sheehy (Bantam). Influential US bestseller which charts the way people change in the course of their lives and how this affects their conduct and their relationships.

The Shattered Dream: Employment in the Eighties, R. Allen et al (Arrow Books). A sane, clearly written and politically unbiased account of the background of the unemployment problem, with an analysis of its various causes and some sensible suggestions for what the government should do about them.

The Third Wave, A. Toffler (Collins). An extremely stimulating look (by the author of the better known *Future Shock*) at how the new technology is shaping the future of work. Good background reading for the more intellectual type of interview.

Reference

Executive Grapevine, (Robert Baird Publications). A comprehensive directory of UK executive search (headhunting) firms and selection consultants. Gives details of their specialities, the salary ranges they deal in, how their fees are calculated and the names of the principles involved. Unfortunately now out of print, but you may get it from your library.

Local Initiatives in Great Britain, Stan Windass (New Foundations for Local Initiative Support). A new and useful directory of organisations providing guidance for the formation of small businesses at local levels.

Useful Addresses

Career Consultants

No complete register of career consultants has been published, but the following is a representative selection in alphabetical order. Several of these firms, it should be noted, also maintain offices outside London.

Career Analysts, Career House, 90 Gloucester Place, London W1 (01-935 5452)

CEPEC (Centre for Professional and Executive Career Development and Counselling), Sundridge Park Management Centre, Bromley, Kent BR1 3JW (01-464 4121)

Chusid, 35-37 Fitzroy Street, London W1P 5AF (01-580 6771)

Connaught Executive Management Services Ltd., 53 Grosvenor Street, London W1X 0DU (01-493 8504)

Percy Coutts & Co. Ltd., 25 Whitehall, London SW1A 2BT (01-839 2271)

Executive Standby (South) Ltd., Office 91, London Wool and Fruit Exchange, Brushfield Street, London E1 (01-247 5693)

Forty Plus Career Development Centre Ltd., High Holborn House, 49-51 Bedford Row, London WC1V 6RL (01-242 4875)

Interexec, Landseer House, 19 Charing Cross Road, London WC2H 0ES (01-930 5041)

John L. Kellett Associates, The Mount, Pinckneys Green, nr Maidenhead, Berks (06284 2097)

Minster Executive Ltd., 28 Bolton Street, London W1Y 8HB (01-493 1309)

MSL Ltd., 17 Stratton Street, London W1X 6DB (01-493 3551)

Sanders & Sidney Ltd., 5-6 Yarmouth Place, Brick Street, London W1Y 7DW (01-492 0491)

Search & Assessment Services Ltd., 1 Garrick House, Carrington Street, London W1Y 7LF (01-499 0321)

Registers
The principal commercial one is generally considered to be:

The Lansdowne Appointments Register, Lansdowne Recruitment, Park House, 207 The Vale, London W3 QB (01-743 6321)

Financial Consultants
The following firm is recommended by the Institute of Directors for its advice on financial and tax problems related to redundancy and severance:

Douglas Deakin Young Ltd., 18 Pall Mall, London SW1 5LV (01-839 2718)

Executive Search Consultants (Headhunters)
The directory publication, *Executive Grapevine* (Baird Publishing Ltd., now out of print) contains particulars of some 200 headhunting firms, including a useful breakdown by speciality, but the principal ones are reckoned to be:

Canny Bowen Associates Ltd., 83 Pall Mall, London SW1Y 5ES (01-839 2561)

Boyden International Ltd., 148 Buckingham Palace Road, London SW1W 9TR (01-730 5292)

Egon Zehnder International, 87 Jermyn Street, London SW1Y 6JD (01-930 9311)

Eurosurvey Ltd., 43/44 Albemarle Street, London W1X 3FE (01-409 1361)
Heidrick and Struggles International, 25-28 Old Burlington Street, London W1X 2BD (01-734 9091)

Hoggett Bowers & Partners Ltd., Sutherland House, 5/6 Argyll Street, London W1E 6E2 (01-734 6852)

Korn Ferry International, 2/4 King Street, London SW1Y 6QL (01-930 5524)

Robin Marlar & Associates Ltd., 14 Grosvenor Place, London SW1X 7HH (01-235 9614/0111)

MSL Executive Search Ltd., 52 Grosvenor Gardens, London SW1W 0AW (01-730 0255)

Russell Reynolds Associates Inc., 1 Mount Street, London W1Y 5AA (01-491 7877)

Spencer Stuart & Associates, Brook House, Park Lane, London W1Y 4HJ (01-492 3866)

John Stork and Partners, 20 Haymarket, London SW1Y 4BP (01-839 4953)

Tyzack & Partners, 10 Hallam Street, London W1N 6DJ (01-580 2924/7)

Wrightson Wood (UK) Ltd., 12 Grosvenor Place, London SW1X 7HH (01-245 9871)

Temporary Executive Jobs Agencies
Manpower Ltd., National Westminster House, The Grove, Slough SL1 1QD

Intex, 53/64 Chancery Lane, London WC2A 1QU

Executive Standby (South) Ltd., 91 Fruit Exchange, Brushfield Street, London E1

Information on Job Sharing
New Ways to Work, 347a Upper Street, London N1 (01-226 4026)

Voluntary Work Abroad

Voluntary Service Overseas, 9 Belgrave Square, London SW1 (01-235 5191)

British Executive Service Overseas, 116 Pall Mall, London SW1 (01-839 1233)

PER Head Office

Professional and Executive Recruitment, Manpower Services Commission, Moorfoot, Sheffield, S1 4PQ